SHARING

THE LOVE OF CHRIST

WITH YOUR

MUSLIM NEIGHBOUR

Love from Ahmu Devi

SHARING
THE LOVE OF CHRIST
WITH YOUR
MUSLIM NEIGHBOUR

by

Ahmad Agyei

SHARING THE LOVE OF CHRIST WITH YOUR MUSLIM NEIGHBOUR

Copyright © 2002 Ahmad Agyei

This edition 2011

Published by:

Integrity Publishers Inc.
P.O. Box 789,
Wake Forest, NC 27588
U.S.A.
info@integritypublishers.org

ISBN 978-0-9828630-6-0

Printed in the United States of America

CONTENTS

FOREWORD

1 Peter 3:15 (NIV)
But in your hearts set apart Christ as Lord. Always be prepared to give an answer to everyone who asks you to give the reason for the hope that you have. But do this with gentleness and respect.

The purpose of this book is to encourage Christians to share the love of Christ with their Muslim neighbour.

The author has observed that current political events throughout the world have tended to widen the gap of suspicion between Christians and Muslims. Many Christians feel disturbed by the increasing influence of Islam in their countries and communities but are confused as to what action God wants them to take. On the other hand, as the author has travelled around he has met many who have seen the opportunity to extend their Christian witness into these communities but they feel ill equipped and don't know how to proceed.

The author is convinced that this is God's time for the Muslim world and that there is a great harvest to be gathered into God's Kingdom. However, as it was in Jesus' time, so it is today; the labourers are few.

The author's concern then is both to give motivation and direction to those who have yet to catch the vision and to offer information and advice to equip those whom God is calling into this labour of love.

The author wishes to acknowledge with sincere thanks the help of Afua Asantewaa who edited this manuscript.

1

GOD'S HEART FOR MUSLIMS

John 10:16 (NIV)
I have other sheep that are not of this sheep pen. I must
bring them also. They too will listen to my voice, and
there shall be one flock and one shepherd.

Introduction

It is a sad fact that many Christians are ignorant of God's
purposes for the Muslim world. Rather than having God's
heart for the Muslims, they feel threatened and become
hard-hearted towards them. Some see Islam as a threat
which can only be conquered by military might. They have
forgotten that we do not use the weapons of the world (2
Corinthians 10:4) and we are not fighting against flesh and
blood (Ephesians 6:12).

Dear friends, we should not become like Jonah who was resentful and opposed God's command to preach the message of salvation to the people of Nineveh. Because of his prejudice, he wanted them to perish in their sins just as many today wish to see all the Muslims in the world destroyed. Such a spirit is not from God. Have we forgotten so soon how Jesus responded to the disciples James and John when they asked him whether he was going to call fire down from Heaven to destroy the Samaritans who rejected even Jesus himself?

Luke 9:55-56 (NIV footnote)
But Jesus turned and rebuked them. And he said, "You do not know what kind of spirit you are of, for the Son of Man did not come to destroy men's lives but to save them."

The fact that a sect or religious group is opposed to our beliefs does not mean we should hate them and wish to see evil befall them. The spirit of Christ is full of Love. Loving when we are hated is what makes Christians different.

The enmity between Jews and Arabs has its history in the conflict between Sarah and Hagar (Genesis 16:4, 6; 21:9-10) and later the struggle between Isaac and Ishmael (Genesis 21:8-9) and their descendants (Genesis 25:18). Unfortunately, over the years, it has found its way into the current Muslim–Christian polarisation. Today, it has even gone beyond the religious borders into the political arena where the West, symbolising Christianity, is seen to be at loggerheads with the Middle East or the Arab world. Even up until today, the settlement of peace between Jew and Arab seems as elusive as ever.

In this book, an attempt will be made to expose the basis of this so-called polarisation as being fallacious and an orchestrated lie by the Evil One just to keep the Arab world in tight isolation from being reached by the gospel of Jesus Christ. What is even more disturbing is the fact that many Christians have fallen victim to this lie and have become partakers in deepening the gulf between the Christian and the Muslim worlds.

This book also seeks to jolt the Christian stereotype mentality about Arabs (and other Muslims) and present the rightful positive image about these "other sheep" who are currently not part of the flock. This in turn will provide us with the correct perspective and incentive based on God's agape love, to reach out to Arabs and Muslims who basically are of the same kindred and must be shown the only way to pass through the gate into the sheepfold

The Sons of Abraham

In reading the book of Genesis we are told:

Genesis 25:7-10 (NIV)
Altogether, Abraham lived a hundred and seventy-five years. Then Abraham breathed his last and died at a good old age, an old man and full of years; and he was gathered to his people. His sons Isaac and Ishmael buried him in the cave of Machpelah near Mamre, in the field of Ephron son of Zohar the Hittite.

This verse clearly demonstrates the fact that on the death of Abraham, Isaac and Ishmael came together to bury him. It is pertinent at this point to ask the question, what can we learn from this verse? I believe sincerely that you will all agree with me that the first identifiable lesson is **love**; the love Isaac had for his brother Ishmael. The second lesson to be learnt is the fact that Isaac monitored every movement of his brother Ishmael so much so that he kept track of him at any point in time. Therefore, when their father Abraham died, he didn't hesitate to inform him for the two to join hands in burying their father, even though Ishmael was **not** the promised child.

Genesis 21:12 (NIV)
"But God said to Abraham, Don't be worried about the boy and your slave Hagar. Do whatever Sarah tells you, because it is through Isaac that your offspring will be reckoned."

In sending away Ishmael, God's promise to Abraham was that he would also make Ishmael into a nation because he was also the offspring of Abraham.

Genesis 21:13 (NIV)
"I will make the son of the maidservant into a nation also, because he is your offspring."

That Ishmael continued in the favour of God is even more explicit in the Genesis 21 incident where God's divine intervention became necessary to provide Hagar with water for her son who was at the point of death. This intervention did not end there for we are told:

Genesis 21:20 (NIV)
God was with the boy as he grew up. He lived in the desert and became an archer.

Despite this Biblical evidence, some who profess to be Christians have argued that Ishmael was an illegitimate child (they even use the offensive term, "bastard") and that his descendants (Arabs and Muslims) are therefore to be regarded in the same light as outcasts. On these grounds, they refuse to consider them as worthy recipients of the gospel. A closer look at the relevant passages will show that they have grossly distorted the truth of God's word.

First, we should note that the fact that Hagar was a maidservant did not make Ishmael an illegitimate child. We can support this assertion by examining the case of Jacob's children. In Genesis 29: 32–30:24; 35:16-26 we are told how Jacob, the younger twin son of Isaac, gave birth to his 12 sons by four different women. Two of these women were the maidservants of the other two, Rachel and Leah, who were the wives Jacob married according to custom. It is recorded that in the case of the maidservants, it was the wives they served who gave them respectively to Jacob as his wives to conceive children on their behalf. This is exactly what Sarah also did in giving her maidservant Hagar to Abraham as a wife. The thing to note is that although four of Jacob's sons were given birth to by his wives' maidservants, two each, yet they were counted together with the rest of their brothers to form the twelve tribes of the nation Israel. The children of the maidservants were not considered as outcasts. Thus it is also quite evident that although Ishmael was not the "promised son," he was never rejected as an outcast. Isaac did not see him as "his enemy" or inferior in spite of the gap between them in their inheritance.

This argument if further supported by Galatians 4:22 which states that Abraham had two sons. Is it true that Abraham **only** had 2 sons? From Genesis 25:1, we see that Abraham took another wife, whose name was Keturah and she also bore him six sons. However, we are told that on the death of Abraham, only two of his sons, namely Isaac and Ishmael, came to together to bury him. Does the word of God then contradict itself? The answer is, "**No**." The first chapter of 1 Chronicles contains the genealogy of Abraham. It gives the names of the sons of Abraham as Isaac and Ishmael (verse 28). Later (in verse 32) it also gives the names of the other six sons, but in contrast to Isaac and Ishmael, they are not identified as the sons of Abraham but rather as, "The sons born to Keturah, Abraham's concubine."

It seems that as far as Bible history is concerned both Isaac and Ishmael and only Isaac and Ishmael are to be recognised as the sons of Abraham. That Ishmael is recognised in this way along with Isaac again stands against any idea of himself or his descendants being outcasts.

Further study shows that in God's plan of salvation, Ishmael becomes the type of those born in the natural way who are enslaved to the law whereas Isaac represents **the children of promise** who are born spiritually having been set free from the law by Christ. Surprisingly, when teaching on this matter (Galations 4:21-31), Paul even identifies the Jews of his generation, physical descendants of Isaac, with Ishmael the son of the slave woman, Hagar.

> **Galatians 4:25 (NIV)**
> Now Hagar stands for Mount Sinai in Arabia and corresponds to the present city of Jerusalem, because she is in slavery with her children.

The reason is that anyone (whether Jew, Gentile or Arab) who tries through their own effort to keep the letter of the Law of God becomes a slave to that law. On the other hand, anyone (whether Jew, Gentile or Arab) who receives Jesus Christ is set free from the curse of the Law and is born by the power of the Spirit and thus becomes a child of the promise. That means that it is not by physical descent but rather by receiving Jesus Christ that one becomes one of the offspring of Abraham and an heir of the blessing that God promised to him.

Galatians 3:26–29 (NIV)
"You are all sons of God through faith in Christ Jesus, for all of you who were baptised into Christ have clothed yourselves with Christ. There is neither Jew nor Greek, slave nor free, male nor female, for you are all one in Christ Jesus. If you belong to Christ, then you are Abraham's seed, and heirs according to the promise."

This however, is no cause for pride, for indeed, in Romans 1:16; 11:11; 11:17–19, the Apostle Paul emphasises that none of the Gentiles were originally included in God's people. However, God in His own mercy and grace through Christ Jesus, has grafted Gentile believers in to become part and parcel of the vine. And we all know that when we talk of "grafting-in" in agricultural science, it implies the process of cutting part of a plant, especially the branch, and fixing it into a cut made in another stronger plant. In this way the stronger species will support the growth of the weaker species; for example, the grafting of a branch of orange into a lime stem.

If we Gentile Christians on this basis claim to be as much the descendants of Abraham as Jewish Christians and consider Abraham to be our father, then we must recognise that Ishmael and his descendants have a more direct inheritance from Abraham than we, the rest of the Gentiles. It is by faith that Abraham has become our father. I should then NOT boast and cast insinuations on the physical descendants of Abraham whether they be Jew or Arab.

The Other Sheep

There is some debate about the meaning of "other sheep" in the passage quoted from John 10:16 at the beginning of this chapter. One school of thought assumes the "other sheep" to mean the Gentiles while another school of thought seeks to argue for something different from the Gentiles. Notwithstanding, the divergence in opinion, it is my prayer that the Holy Spirit shall guide our hearts and minds as we proceed to examine what is written in the Bible. Our task, therefore in this section, is to identify the "other sheep" and have them brought into the pen.

In Genesis 25:13-16, we are told that Ishmael gave birth to 12 sons who became tribal rulers. Their names were Nebaioth, Kedar, Midirin, Mishma, Dumah, Massa, Hadad, Tema, Jetur, Naphish and Kedemah. Of these sons, the reader should keep in mind the name of the first two, Nebaioth and Kedar. Just as Jacob, having obtained the blessing of his father Isaac, gave birth to 12 sons from whom came the 12 tribes of Israel, so Ishmael also gave birth to 12 sons who became the heads of the 12 Ishmaelite or Arab tribes. These were included among "the nations" referred to so many times throughout the Bible.

In his prophecies, Isaiah shows how the nations would be drawn to worship God. He names specific nations and it may surprise the reader to see that these include nations that are currently well known as Islamic nations. Consider the following:

Isaiah 60:6 (NIV)
…And all from **Sheba** will come, bearing gold and incense and proclaiming the praise of the LORD.

Sheba is present-day Yemen and this prophecy declares that all her people will come with gifts to praise the Lord.

Isaiah 19:23-25 (NIV)
In that day there will be a highway from Egypt to Assyria. The Assyrians will go to Egypt and the Egyptians to Assyria. The Egyptians and Assyrians will worship together. In that day Israel will be the third, along with Egypt and Assyria, a blessing on the earth. The LORD Almighty will bless them, saying, "Blessed be **Egypt** my people, **Assyria** my handiwork, and Israel my inheritance."

In this remarkable prophecy, Egypt and Assyria are mentioned in the same breath as Israel as being equally God's people. The titles "my people," "my handiwork" and "my inheritance" had previously belonged exclusively to Israel but this prophecy made it clear that any nation who comes to worship God is to be counted as God's people. We all know that current day Egypt is predominately an Islamic nation. Assyria too can be identified as being made up from parts of the current nations of Turkey, Iraq and Syria, all of which are well known as Islamic nations.

More specifically, Isaiah prophesied about the very descendants of Ishmael:

Isaiah 42:11-12 (NIV)
Let the desert and its towns raise their voices; let the settlements where **Kedar** lives rejoice. Let the people of Sela sing for joy; let them shout from the mountaintops. Let them give glory to the LORD and proclaim his praise in the islands.

As we have already seen, Kedar was the second-born son of Ishmael and his descendants formed one of the 12 Ishmaelite tribes. His descendants are seen rejoicing and praising the Lord.

Isaiah 60:7 (NIV)
All **Kedar's** flocks will be gathered to you, the rams of **Nebaioth** will serve you; they will be accepted as offerings on my altar, and I will adorn my glorious temple.

This prophecy also includes Nebaioth, the first-born son of Ishmael along with Kedar. It show that their descendants will come to minister in the Temple of God together with the sons of Jacob. Note that here they are referred to as sheep, the same word Jesus used in John 10:16. This shows that the heart-beat of God was clearly towards the salvation of these people and that they should also be brought into the Temple to worship Him. There was no doubt that Isaiah was an outstanding prophet of the Bible. Therefore, it is very important that we take his word of prophecy very seriously.

Since Muslims identify themselves as the descendants of Ishmael in the same way that Christians identify themselves as the descendants of Abraham and Israel, they must surely be included in these Biblical prophecies. Thus we must conclude that the Bible clearly anticipates a day when the descendants of Ishmael and other Muslims will come to worship God and be counted among His people.

Can Ishmaelites and Muslims stand on these prophecies to claim access into the Kingdom of God? After all, Muslims may argue that they are worshipping God and therefore that these prophecies have already been fulfilled. However, they address God as Allah, they do not know Him by His personal name "Yahweh" (Jehovah) which is translated LORD in the prophecies quoted above. These prophecies are clear that the people will come to worship the LORD (Yahweh), this implies that they have a personal relationship with Him.

The Bible shows very clearly that there is only one way to enter into such a personal relationship with the LORD God and that way is very specific-they must be called and gathered by the Shepherd.

The Shepherd

If we take the time to study the Biblical basis for mission to the nations, we shall see how God's plan of salvation unfolded from the time of Abraham. God called Abraham to go and promised to bless him and his descendants and to make them a blessing to the nations.

> **Genesis 12:1-3 (NIV)**
> The LORD had said to Abram, "Leave your country, your people and your father's household and go to the land I will show you. I will make you into a great nation and I will bless you; I will make your name great, and you will be a blessing. I will bless those who bless you, and whoever curses you I will curse; and **all peoples on earth will be blessed through you.**"

God revealed Himself as Yahweh ("I AM" Exodus 3:14-15) to the nation of Israel. Since they were the descendants of Abraham through Isaac, He wanted them to act as priests for the rest of the nations.

> **Exodus 19:5-6 (NIV)**
> "...Now if you obey me fully and keep my covenant, then out of all nations you will be my treasured

possession. Although the whole earth is mine, you will be for me a kingdom of priests and a holy nation."

The main duties of priests are to show people God's way, by bringing His word to them, and to bring people to God. God intended that Israel should be a holy nation who would show the nations what God required through her actions. It was His desire that in this way, the nations would come to worship Him and receive His blessing.

Deuteronomy 4:5-8 (NIV)
See, I have taught you decrees and laws as the LORD my God commanded me, so that you may follow them in the land you are entering to take possession of it. Observe them carefully, for this will show your wisdom and understanding to the nations, who will hear about all these decrees and say, "Surely this great nation is a wise and understanding people." What other nation is so great as to have their gods near them the way the LORD our God is near us whenever we pray to him? And what other nation is so great as to have such righteous decrees and laws as this body of laws I am setting before you today?

Even the Qur'an recognises the fact that the Jews were looked upon with special favour:

Qur'an 2:47
O Children of Israel! Call to mind the (special) favor which I bestowed upon you, and that I preferred you to all others.

Tragically, Israel failed in her task because she followed the ways of the nations and became disobedient and unfaithful to God. Thus she destroyed her own testimony.

However, Isaiah prophesied of one who would come to fulfil the task that God gave to Israel.

Isaiah 11:1-2, 10 (NIV)
A shoot will come up from the stump of Jesse; from his roots a Branch will bear fruit. The Spirit of the LORD will rest on him--the Spirit of wisdom and of understanding, the Spirit of counsel and of power, the Spirit of knowledge and of the fear of the LORD--...In that day the Root of Jesse will stand as a banner for the peoples; the nations will rally to him, and his place of rest will be glorious.

Verses 3-5 indicate that he would rule as a king. The reference to Jesse indicates that he would not just be another king in the line of David, but rather that he would be another David for only David is referred to as the son of Jesse.

This ties in with other prophecies that God would raise up another David.

Jeremiah 30:9 (NIV)
Instead, they will serve the LORD their God and David their king, whom I will raise up for them.

As we know, David was a shepherd before he became a king and therefore we should not be surprised to learn that the new David would also be a shepherd.

Ezekiel 34:23-24
And I will set up one Shepherd over them, and He shall feed them, even My servant David. He shall feed them, and He shall be their Shepherd. And I, the LORD, will be their God, and My servant David a prince among them. I, the LORD, have spoken it.

Ezekiel 37:24
And David My Servant shall be King over them, and they all shall have one Shepherd…

God gives this new David the title "My Servant" and thus we can identify him as the Servant spoken of in Isaiah.

Isaiah 42:1, 6-7
"Behold My Servant, whom I uphold, Mine Elect, in whom My soul delighteth: I have put My Spirit upon Him; He shall bring forth judgment to the Gentiles… I, the LORD, have called Thee in righteousness, and will hold Thine hand, and will keep Thee, and give Thee for a covenant of the people, for a light of the Gentiles; to open the blind eyes, to bring out the prisoners from the prison, and them that sit in darkness out of the prison house."

Isaiah 49:6
He said, "It is a light thing that Thou shouldest be My servant to raise up the tribes of Jacob and to restore the preserved of Israel. I will also give Thee for a light to the Gentiles, that Thou mayest be My salvation unto the end of the earth."

Note that God further identifies the one who would gather the nations as "My (God's) salvation."

There is only one who was qualified to be the Shepherd and his identity becomes very clear when we look at how the Old Testament prophecies were fulfilled in the New Testament.

In the words of Simeon, the old man who blessed Jesus as a baby on the day of his dedication to God, Luke shows that the one who would draw the nations to himself was no less a person than Jesus.

Luke 2:30-32 (NIV)
"...For my eyes have seen **your salvation**, which you have prepared in the sight of all people, **a light for revelation to the Gentiles** and for glory to your people Israel..."

Jesus also fully identifies himself as the "Good Shepherd" who would gather the sheep:

John 10:11,14 (NIV)
"I am the Good Shepherd; the Good Shepherd lays down his life for the sheep... I am the good shepherd; I know my sheep and my sheep know me –"

Let's read what Jesus, who foresaw the advent of "other sheep" coming into the fold, says in John 10 verses 1 and 7. In verse 1, Jesus confirms the existence of other sheep who must come into the pen. However, he stresses the point that the gate is the **only way** by which they can enter the pen. The one who tries to find another way to enter is identified as thief or a robber.

To find which gate Jesus was referring to, we need to turn to the verse 7 of John 10. Here Jesus unambiguously claims to be the only gate by which the sheep may enter the pen. He opens the way by laying down his life for the sheep and they show their response by listening to his voice. They will come when he calls them.

Our Task

As Jesus was to be a light to the nations so his followers are to continue this ministry.

Matthew 28:19 (NIV)
Then Jesus came to them and said, "All authority in heaven and on earth has been given to me. Therefore **go and make disciples of all nations,** baptising them in the name of the Father and of the Son and of the Holy Spirit, and teaching them to obey everything I have commanded you. And surely I am with you always, to the very end of the age."

The Apostle Paul in particular was given this commission:

Acts 9:15 (NIV)
But the Lord said to Ananias, "Go! This man (Paul) is my chosen instrument to carry my name before the Gentiles and their kings and before the people of Israel..."

Acts 13:47 (NIV)
"For this is what the Lord has commanded us: 'I have made you a light for the Gentiles, that you may bring salvation to the ends of the earth.'"

Luke wrote the book of Acts to show how the early disciples fulfilled the commission of their Lord to bring salvation to the ends of the earth, that is to the all the nations. This is summarised in the following verse:

Acts 1:8 (NIV)
"But you will receive power when the Holy Spirit comes on you; and you will be my witnesses in Jerusalem, and in all Judea and Samaria, and to the ends of the earth."

In the plan of God, this empowerment by the Holy Spirit happened on the Day of Pentecost when people from all nations had gathered at Jerusalem to celebrate the festival and worship God in the Jewish way. These peoples represented the different nations to whom the gospel was to be taken. Thus it is important for us to note who was there.

Acts 2:9-11 (NIV)
"Parthians, Medes and Elamites; residents of Mesopotamia, Judea and Cappadocia, Pontus and Asia, Phrygia and Pamphylia, **Egypt** and the parts of **Libya** near Cyrene; visitors from Rome (both Jews and converts to Judaism); Cretans and **Arabs**-- we hear them declaring the wonders of God in our own tongues!"

Arabs are specifically named along with citizens of other countries and regions which are now Islamic states such as Libya, Egypt and Asia. Thus the argument that such nations are outside of God's plan of salvation simply cannot hold.

Furthermore, in 2 Corinthians 5:18-20, Paul says that our Lord has committed to us a ministry of reconciliation. Reconciliation simply implies bringing together two or more parties who are at loggerheads. This can only be achieved in a spirit of love and brotherliness.

2 Corinthians 5:18-20. (NIV)
All this is from God, who reconciled us to himself through Christ and gave us the ministry of reconciliation: that God was reconciling the world to himself in Christ, not counting men's sins against them. And he has committed to us the message of reconciliation. We are therefore Christ's ambassadors, as though God were making his appeal through us. We implore you on Christ's behalf: Be reconciled to God. God made him who had no sin to be sin for us, so that in him we might become the righteousness of God.

This ministry of reconciliation is firstly to bring the Muslims into a personal relationship with God through Jesus Christ and secondly to reconcile them to the rest of God's people. Then all the sheep will become one with one shepherd just as the prophecies have foretold.

Let me ask you this question. Why is it that it is Paul who unearths this revelation? Perhaps we will find the answer in Paul's own testimony:

Galatians 1:15-19 (NIV)
But when God, who set me apart from birth and called me by His Grace, was pleased to reveal His Son in me so that I might preach Him among the Gentiles, I did not consult any man nor did I go up to Jerusalem to see those who were apostles before I was, **but I went immediately into Arabia** and later returned to Damascus. Then after three years, I went up to Jerusalem to get acquainted with Peter and stayed with him fifteen days. I saw none of the other apostles-only James, the Lord's brother.

This passage reveals the heart of God towards the Arabs. Paul did not consult any man but went straight to Arabia after his conversion. He does not mince any words but states clearly that he was led there by the Spirit of God. So may the Spirit of God also lead you to awaken the conscience of our Muslims brothers and sisters to Christ in the Spirit of love and brotherliness.

Thus we must conclude that far from being outcasts, God has a special heart to draw the descendants of Ishmael to himself through Jesus. In fact, all the evidence in the world today suggests that this is indeed God's strategic time to bring salvation to the Muslims. We should not therefore be surprised to see that Satan is doing all in his power to alienate people from Muslims and to stir up hatred against them. His aim is to keep their eyes blinded and to stop them from hearing the truth of the gospel of God's salvation in Jesus Christ. We, as Christians, must beware of Satan's schemes and not allow our hearts to be hardened towards Muslims.

Rather, than seeing the rise of Islam as a threat we should see it as a challenge to be part of what God is doing among them. If we see Muslims moving into our communities we should thank God for the opportunity. For the Bible teaches that it was God who planned the movements of all peoples. He determined the times of their movements and the exact places where they should live and He did this in order that some of them would seek for Him and find Him (Acts 17:26-27).

Some Christians have also by-passed mission to the Muslims on the grounds that they are too hardened and set in their ways to turn to Christ. Some too, are afraid to cause offence because our modern world teaches that everyone has the right to his own belief and that there are different ways to worship the same God. All these are further lies from Satan to keep Muslims from hearing the truth of the gospel. Indeed, experience shows that there is a spiritual hunger among many Muslims and that they are actively searching for the truth. Christ has even appeared to some in visions and they are seeking for those who can explain what they have seen. Let us then be encouraged by the prophecies because we know that whatever God has promised will be fulfilled.

The Bible then is clear that we as the followers of Jesus have to continue His task of bringing light to the Gentiles and especially to the Muslims so that all the sheep may be gathered in.

> **Romans 10:12-15 ((NIV)**
> For there is no difference between Jew and Gentile--the same Lord is Lord of all and richly blesses all who call on him, for, "Everyone who calls on the name of the Lord (Jesus) will be saved." How, then, can they call on the one they have not believed in? And how can they believe in the one of whom they have not heard? And how can they hear without someone preaching to them? And how can they preach unless they are sent? As it is written, "How beautiful are the feet of those who bring good news!"

Amen!

2

A MUSLIM TURNS TO CHRIST

How I Was Converted

When I was in Islam, I thought that both Christians and Muslims served the same God, but with differences in approach. We were made to believe in all the prophets without any distinction.

In Islam, adherents of the faith worship and follow Allah. Muhammad was a mere messenger. There is therefore nowhere in the Qur'an that Muslims are called upon to follow Muhammad. As a result Muslims are not Muhammadans.

Islam also teaches that Jesus was one of the greatest prophets of Allah but his mission ended with his ascension to heaven. Therefore, we are now in the era of the Prophet of Islam who is supposed to be the last of the prophets.

However, in the course of reading the Qur'an I came across certain statements which Allah had revealed but which raised serious questions in my mind:

Qur'an 57:27
We sent after them Jesus the son of Mary, and bestowed on him the Gospel; and We ordained in the hearts of those who followed him Compassion and Mercy.

Qur'an 3:55
Behold! Allah said: "O Jesus! I will take thee and raise thee to Myself and clear thee (of the falsehoods) of those who blaspheme; I will make those who follow thee superior to those who reject faith, to the Day of Resurrection:"

In these two Qur'anic verses, Allah allows Jesus to have followers whom He has blessed with compassion and mercy and who are also exalted above those who disbelieve in Jesus until the Day of Resurrection. This verse also reveals that the mission of Jesus will not end until the Day of Resurrection.

I decided to research further and came across Sura 61:6 and 10:94. In Sura 61: 6, Jesus predicted the coming of Muhammad after him:

Qur'an 61:6
And remember, Jesus, the son of Mary, said: "O Children of Israel! I am the apostle of Allah (sent) to you, confirming the Law (which came) before me, and giving Glad Tidings of an Apostle to come after me, whose name shall be Ahmad."

and in 10:94, Allah told Muhammad that if he was in doubt about what had been revealed to him, he should ask those who had been reading "the Book," which I understood to be the Bible:

Qur'an 10:94
If thou wert in doubt as to what We have revealed unto thee, then ask those who have been reading the Book from before

thee: The Truth hath indeed come to thee from thy Lord: So
be in no wise of those in doubt.

I got confused at this stage. So I contacted my college
mates who were Christians in the Scripture Union, to ask
whether Muhammad's name is in the Bible. But they said,
"No." They went on further to state that Christianity and
Islam are not the same and unless one confesses Jesus as his
Lord and Saviour, that person cannot be saved. However, as
a Muslim, I also knew that unless you recite the **Kalimatu-
Shahada** – "there is no other God but Allah and I bear
witness that Muhammad is his messenger"- and practise
the remaining five pillars you are not saved.

In my state of confusion I decided to pray to God to
direct me. While praying I said, "God, I am not going to
consult any Reverend Minister to direct me. If you do not
tell me the truth and I die, and you later tell me, 'Ahmad,
you were on the wrong track and therefore you will go to
hell', I will say 'God, when I was on the earth I asked you to
show me the right way, but you did not.' "

I made a three-day fast to wait on God for an answer to
my request. It was during this period that the Lord revealed
Himself to me through a dream during the night. While I
was sleeping, I dreamt that I had been surrounded by some
prophets who were saying to me, "a Christian, a man of
God." It was around midnight when the dream occurred
and I woke up and asked myself, "how can a Muslim have
such a dream?" However, the next morning, something
made me understand that the dream was an answer to my
prayer.

Because of this I become double minded. I could
neither pray in the Muslim way nor the Christian way. So
I became what I termed "MusChri" meaning half Muslim
and half Christian! This went on for sometime and then one

night while asleep I heard a small still voice warning me that if I did not stop what I was doing and surrender my life completely to Jesus Christ, something terrible would happen to me. I woke up and again saw that it was midnight. I readily knelt down, prayed and finally surrendered my life to the Lord. That was in 1983.

I know you will ask how can a Muslim pray this way? However, the Bible reveals that God says:

Jeremiah 29:12-13
Then shall ye call upon Me, and ye shall go and pray unto Me and I will hearken unto you. And ye shall seek Me and find Me when ye shall search for Me with all your heart.

Psalm 50:15 (NIV)
…call upon me in the day of trouble, I will deliver you and you will honour me.

Around this same time my father had obtained a passport for me and completed arrangements for me to study abroad but it was not to be.

Cursed By My Father

When my father, who was a hard-line Muslim, realised that I had become a Christian, he called me before the whole family and ordered me to forsake my new found faith in Christ Jesus. When I refused, he ordered me out of his house with a curse. He said, "Ahmad, mark it on the wall this day; throughout your life, you will never prosper in this world." My reply to him was, "the one in me is greater than the one in you,"

To survive, I was hopping about from one friend's place to another. How to get something to eat became a big problem. Finally, I became somebody's labourer for 3 years, taking care of 80 sheep and goats and 1500 birds. Poultry farming for my master. Three years in the Lord with hard labour!

God's programme for developing maturity in the life of the believer, without exception, includes trials and testings. This is not the curriculum the new convert elects, but the prescribed course from the Master Teacher.

The Lord taught His disciples:

Matthew 7:13,14
"…wide is the gate and broad is the way that leadeth to destruction, and many there be which go in thereat. Because straight is the gate and **narrow** is the way, which leadeth unto life, and few there are that find it"

The word "narrow" used here comes from the Greek verb *thlibo* which means to press, afflict or distress. This clearly indicates that the Lord's school to lead His own on to spiritual maturity will require the disciple to undergo oppression and affliction.

The apostle Paul taught his new converts the same truth. He doubled back to all the cities of his first missionary journey:

Acts 14:22
…confirming the souls of the disciples, and exhorting them to continue in the faith, and that we must, through much tribulation, enter into the Kingdom of God.

Since the word promises that God is working out all things for the believer's good and for His glory, it is obvious that the trials are designed to produce blessing, not bitterness, in the life of the believer.

The Curse Turns Into Blessing

Despite my father's curse, the Lord has been blessing me because God's word declares that:

Proverbs 26:2
As the bird by wandering, as a swallow by flying, so a curse without cause shall not alight.

Seven years after the curse, my father called me back home. He had been watching me and had seen that there had been a dramatic change in my life for the better. This was the work of Christ in my life. My father asked me to forgive him and promised to visit my family. Later he surrendered himself to the Lord Jesus, and my mother is also now a born-again Christian. In addition, out of my father's thirty-one children, two-thirds have come to a saving knowledge of Jesus Christ. When my father died in 1992, even though I was not the oldest son, it was I who was nominated by the family to file the letter of administration at the Regional High Court. It was granted and later the properties of my father were shared among us.

As a result of my testimony, many other Muslims were encouraged to turn to Christ because they were no longer afraid of the power of curses on their lives.

3

TRIALS OF THE NEW CONVERT

Introduction

Most Muslim converts go through severe trials as a result of their new faith in Christ. It is hoped that this chapter will provide encouragement for those suffering in this way and will give other Christians a better understanding so that they can provide the right sort of help.

The word "trial" as used in the New Testament originates from the Greek words *dokimē* and *dokimion*. These words carry the meaning of a test, examination, experiment or proof and in the Bible it is the Christian's faith which is their object. They carry almost the same meaning as the equivalent word in Hebrew, *bachan*. This is the word used of the trial of Job (34:36). In his case, the source of temptation was Satan but even so, it was only by God's permission that Satan was allowed to act. The Bible shows that trials are not meant to tear us away from

God but rather they are to help us know God better. Mind you, trials are different from temptations. Temptations are strategies and plans designed and purported by Satan to cause us to sin and thus to separate us from God. Therefore, we have every cause to be angry and resist Satan and all the temptations he brings our way. Trials, on the other hand, help to draw us closer to God and to become stronger in our faith.

Where Do Trials Come From?

We now know that it is Satan who brings temptation on Christians. Who then brings tests and trials into the life of the Christian? Is it God or Satan? It is popular thinking to shift the blame onto the devil for every pain and suffering we experience as Christians. Sometimes the devil may indeed be involved in our tests and trials, however, the Psalmist has a different story to tell:

Psalm 11:5
The LORD trieth the righteous...

From this psalm, tests and trials come from who? God. In fact, Job never attributed his suffering and pain to Satan, even though he was in fact being attacked by Satan. He intentionally refused to acknowledge Satan in any of his trying moments. He knew he was dealing with God.

We must know that in our trials we are either dealing with God or sometimes it is simply because of our own misdeeds. We should stop giving Satan unnecessary honour by making him the author of all our trials. For whenever we put the blame on him, self-pity sets in, fear grips us and we feel so unfortunate. The result of all this is that we tend to run away from further trials. However, we can never run away from trials forever. Even if we manage to do so today, we shall meet them again tomorrow. So the earlier we begin to endure trials patiently, the better.

It is an established fact that whosoever accepts Christ in truth as Saviour and Lord will go through trials of a sort. It is very disturbing that many preachers of our generation go about telling Christians, especially new converts, that the Christian walk is rosy and easy, full of gold and buttered bread. For with time, this fake promise becomes an illusion and some of these naïve converts become troubled and distressed. They start to think that God hates them and that this is the reason why they are not having the gold and bread they were promised by these unscrupulous preachers. With this thinking they then tend to leave the faith. However, Christ Himself never promised us a trouble-free Christian life. For He said,

Matthew 10:21-22
Brother will betray brother to death and a father his child; children will rebel against their parents and have them put to death. All men will hate you because of Me, but he who stands firm to the end will be saved.

The Lord is teaching us from this passage that trials and persecutions shall come upon us right after we have declared Him as Lord and Master. Unbelievably, they shall come from people of our own homes. The people who once loved us and cherished us:

1 Peter 4:3-4
For you have spent enough time in the past doing what pagans choose to do--living in debauchery, lust, drunkenness, orgies, carousing and detestable

idolatry. They think it strange that you do not plunge with them into the same flood of dissipation, and they heap abuse on you.

Trials are not meant to kill us so we should not be surprised when the "fiery trials" come our way as though something strange were happening to us (1 Peter 4:12). Rather:

James 1:2-4
Consider it pure joy, my brothers, whenever you face trials of many kinds, because you know that the testing of your faith develops perseverance. Perseverance must finish its work so that you may be mature and complete, not lacking anything.

Do we want to grow into maturity? Do we want to be complete, lacking nothing? I believe the answers are positive, "Yes". Then why do we want to run away from trials? Let us abide under the shadow of trials for:

2 Timothy 3:12 (NIV)
In fact, everyone who wants to live a godly life in Christ Jesus will be persecuted,

Trials Turn To Blessing

Matthew 5: 10-12 (NIV)
Blessed are those who are persecuted because of righteousness, for theirs is the kingdom of heaven. "Blessed are you when people insult you, persecute you

and falsely say all kinds of evil against you because of me. Rejoice and be glad, because great is your reward in heaven, for in the same way they persecuted the prophets who were before you.

It is clearly spelt out that as new converts, trials, persecutions and sufferings are to bless us, strengthen us and keep us grounded in our new found faith. The benefits of trials include:

- Causing us to persevere so that we do not fall out of the faith (James 1:2-4).
- To humble, teach and discipline us and thereby make us available for every good work (Deuteronomy 8:2-5).
- To refine us and make us honourable vessels for the Master's use. (Psalm 66:10).
- To check our foundation in Christ and to ascertain whether we are deeply or superficially rooted in Christ (1 Corinthians 3:10-15).
- To strengthen our faith (1 Peter 1:6-7).
- To enable us to be overcomers (Revelation 2&3).
- To cause God's power to increase in us (Psalm 102:23).
- To separate the chosen from the called (Isaiah 48:10)

It is important to know that trials may come in diverse form. However, whatever the case may be, we should rest assured that they are meant for our good.

The Greatest Trial

With my background as a Muslim-convert, I can personally attest to the fact that the greatest trial to every

Muslim-convert is rejection by their family and expulsion from their home. Those in school may have their education terminated and others may lose their job. If a man gets converted, his wife may be taken away from him and if it is a woman, her husband may divorce her and her children may be taken away. These things do not occur in every case, but every convert should be prepared to face such trials. We should be encouraged to know that we are not the first people to go through trying moments. The great chapter of faith, Hebrew 11, reveals that the saints of old were tortured, some faced jeers and flogging, while still others were chained and put in prison. They were stoned, they were sawn in two and they were put to death by the sword. If history reveals the suffering and trials of people like them, who are now resting in the bosom of their father, do we want to be treated less?

Paul says:

Romans 8:18 (NIV)
I consider that our present sufferings are not worth comparing with the glory that will be revealed in us.

If some were prepared to die for the sake of the gospel why should we refuse to endure hunger, thirst, nakedness, sleepless nights, etc. The financial problems should not weigh us down. All we need to do is to stand up and raise our heads to our Father in Heaven in whom there is no shadow of turning. He tells us not to fear the great trial that is come upon us:

Malachi 3:6
"For I am the LORD, I change not. Therefore ye sons of Jacob are not consumed."

The Psalmist could say:

Psalm 121:1-4 (NIV)
I lift up my eyes to the hills--where does my help come from? My help comes from the LORD, the Maker of heaven and earth. He will not let your foot slip--he who watches over you will not slumber; indeed, he who watches over Israel will neither slumber nor sleep.

The Lord will keep you from all harm, - He will watch over your life; the Lord will watch over your coming and going both now and for evermore.

The Role of the Church

In fact, the new convert should expect a trial of a sort from the church members and sometimes from even the Pastor. The behaviour and conduct of some people who claimed to be converted have discouraged some Pastors to the extent that they do not easily give a helping hand to converts. This is because some converts, after they have been rehabilitated, begin to misbehave and indulge in sinful activities. Some have stolen church property, others, after they are settled, do not continue with the Christian faith.

The caution here is that we should stop pampering new converts. The most common mistake in the Christian circles is that we shower gifts, money, etc. on this new convert. Before long, they become greedy. That is why many of them go from church to church sharing their testimonies with the intention of being paid for. They should not be so eager to mount the pulpit or to become leaders for they tend to make merchandise of the grace they have received from God. Eventually, they are destroyed by this foolish act. We should rather, direct new converts to work with their own hands so that they can provide for their needs and the needs of others (Ephesians 4:28). Otherwise, as the Bible warns (2 Thessalonians 3:11-12) there is a danger that they will become lazy, busybodies who lose sight of the goal of their faith.

The church however, must not be too hard on these new converts. There is a balance to be found so that they are not over-stretched beyond what they can bear. I suggest that we institute a "New Convert Care Fund" specifically to help these new converts to become established. It may, for instance, be necessary to provide them with means to train for work or to set up in some business. If we do this, I believe the new converts will be encouraged to stay in the fold and not fall prey to those who would induce them to return to Islam. Paul when leaving Ephesus for good, gave this admonition to the church leaders:

Acts 20:28 (NIV)
Keep watch over yourselves and all the flock of which the Holy Spirit has made you overseers. Be shepherds of the church of God which he bought with his own blood.

We must do our part to keep the new ones and leave the rest to God. He will always honour His part of the task. All we need to do is to ask for direction and strength and I know our labour shall be rewarded, it shall never be in vain.

Encouraging A Right Attitude

After I had been rejected and sacked from home, I went about doing menial jobs despite the fact that I came from a relatively rich home. I cared for sheep, goats and poultry. I had to go out everyday to bring fodder to the flock, clean the pen, draw water for the animals. Then after, I had to clean the house, wash my master's car and do other washing. I did this job for quite a time. At that time I thought I was being maltreated, but now I can testify that the training I had has made me a better person. God was disciplining me as the son He loves. Beloved, do not run away from God's discipline, else, you will become like an illegitimate child, good for nothing. Yes,

> **Hebrews 12:11 (NIV)**
> "No discipline seems pleasant at the time, but painful. Later on, however, it produces a harvest of righteousness and peace for those who have been trained by it."

From now on, develop a right attitude towards trials. A positive attitude towards trials and suffering is the key to the triumphant Christian life. With this attitude, recognise God in the periods of trial but continue to trust Him. Above all, consider trials as working for your good.

4

WITNESSING TO MUSLIMS IN PRACTICE

Prayer is the Key

The spiritual forces behind Islam are very strong and therefore one cannot witness without effective prayer. As Jesus said:

Matthew 12:29 (NIV)
"How can anyone enter a strong man's house and carry off his possessions unless he first ties up the strong man? Then he can rob his house."

As we have already said, we are not fighting a physical battle, but a spiritual one.

Ephesians 6:12 (NIV)
For our struggle is not against flesh and blood, but against rulers, against authorities, against evil powers

of this dark world and against spiritual forces of evil in the heavenly realms.

Therefore, we must put on our spiritual armour (Ephesians 6:13-17) through prayer and we must use it with intense prayer:

Ephesians 6:18 (NIV)
And pray in the Spirit on all occasions with all kinds of prayers and requests.

As we take the gospel to Muslims, we can expect great resistance for:

2 Corinthians 4:4 (NIV)
The god of this age has blinded the minds of unbelievers, so that they cannot see the light of the gospel of the glory of Christ, who is the image of God.

Satan wants to keep Muslims in bondage in order to rob our Lord Jesus Christ of His honour and glory. When a Muslim father names his child, he will sacrifice an animal (traditionally a goat). As he does so, he faces himself and the animal towards the Black Stone (which forms the cornerstone of the Ka'ba in Mecca, see page 96) then, as he cuts the animal's throat, he proclaims the name of the child. In so doing, he believes that he is dedicating the child to Allah. However, we must realise that he is in fact committing the child into a blood covenant with the evil spirit(s) behind the Black Stone. Later in life, if the child makes even one step towards Christ, these spiritual forces will attempt to pull him or her back. Prayer then is essential to break the power of these spirits to whom the Muslim is bound.

One must always keep in mind that conversion is a work of God through His Holy Spirit. No one else has the power the convert a Muslim even if our arguments are convincing and we show love and respect. However, we can be encouraged that, as a result of our prayers, the Holy Spirit will give us the right words to say and with His power, He will make them effective.

2 Corinthians 10:3-5 (NIV)
For though we live in the world, we do not wage war as the world does. The weapons we fight with are not the weapons of the world. On the contrary, they have divine power to demolish strongholds. We demolish arguments and every pretension that sets itself up against the knowledge of God and we take captive every thought to make it obedient to Christ.

The battle will be won on our knees! And not ours only, but with the support of our brothers and sisters in Christ. In this way, the barrier of fear will be demolished and our faith in Christ will be strengthened until our task is accomplished.

Our Attitude

While it is by no means a crime to witness to a Muslim the method employed can be cruel, wicked, unacceptable and in the end fruitless.

Christ who has instructed us to go and witness, has also laid down a method that we must follow and pursue if we truly want to achieve any results. The method is not our method; it is Jesus' method. The method is based on compassion and great love for the lost souls. Whilst on earth, our Lord went through all the towns and villages teaching and preaching the good news of the Kingdom and healing every disease and when he saw the crowds he had compassion on them, because they were harassed and helpless, like sheep without a shepherd.

When we see the Muslims in our communities or on our televisions, how do we feel? Is the feeling one of anger, bitterness, hatred etc? Do we see them as enemies? We need to recognise that it is because of such negative feelings and tendencies that Christians have largely failed to reach Muslims. In fact, it rather seems that it is the Muslims who are going out into every part of the world. In the U.K. many church buildings have been taken over and converted into mosques. Why should this be so? Did Christ not say He would build His church and the gates of Hell would not be able to prevail against it? Why then the seeming defeat of the church? It is because the Christians have failed to do things the way God wants us to do them. We need to repent and change our ways to His.

Jesus sent out his disciples with the following instruction:

Matthew 10:16 (NIV)
"I am sending you out like sheep among wolves. Therefore be as shrewd as snakes and as innocent as doves."

Here the Lord was using symbolism in a parable. A parable is simply a saying that is designed to teach a moral lesson. Therefore, to understand the meaning of this saying we need to look at the trait of the animals that are mentioned:

Animal	Characteristics
Sheep	Submissive, vulnerable and foolish
Dove	Gentle, peaceful and harmless
Wolf	Wild, predatory and savage
Snake (Serpent)	Crafty, subtle and purposeful

Let us note well that a sheep will never succeed if it tries to attack a wolf!

Our Lord meant that, in our witness amongst the Muslims, we need to be obedient -totally dependant on Him and submissive to His commands. He did **not** mean that we should be as foolish as sheep. If we go and behave foolishly, the wolves will take their chance to devour us! They will throw stones at us, beat us and mishandle us. If this happens, we should not claim to be suffering for Christ, because we will rather be suffering for our foolishness. This does not mean that, in our effort to witness about Christ, we shall not suffer but that it should not happen because of our own misbehaviour. We need to recognise that we are vulnerable and defenceless therefore we must not go our own way, but allow Christ to guide us in all we do. There is a balance to be maintained, for the Lord says we should be gentle, calm and innocent as the dove but at the same time we have to be as wise, crafty and purposeful as the snake. It is in this way we will succeed in our task to witness to Muslims.

Some Christians have so much hatred against Muslims to the extent that, in their effort to witness to them, they try to use the wolf's method instead of Jesus'. Let me ask you a question, how do you feel if you hear somebody insulting a person that you hold in high esteem? I believe that, if you are honest, your natural instinct would be to show anger.

In the same way, Muslims are bound to become angry and aggressive if you go about insulting their religion and their prophets.

An Imam once said that if Christians claim to have a message of salvation for the Muslims, they should have a better and nicer way of presenting it rather than attacking and insulting them. Brothers and Sisters, the ball is in our court and we must grasp hold of it. Our master wants us to save souls and not to lose or destroy them for the soul is precious to the Lord. He died for **all** and this includes the Muslims too.

Speaking Words of Peace and Blessing

Another important part of the method that Jesus taught His disciples is to enter a place with words of peace and blessing.

> **Luke 10:5-6 (c.f. Matthew 10:12-13)**
> "When you enter a house, first say, '**Peace be to this house**.' If a man of peace is there, your peace will rest on him; if not, it will return to you."

The Hebrew term for peace – *shalom*, which Jesus would have used, means far more than the absence of war or conflict. It means "well-being" or "wholeness" and it includes every area of life: health, prosperity, security, friendship and salvation. To utter this word of greeting is therefore to speak blessing into the lives of those who receive the greeting. It was the greeting that was (and still is) used by the Jews and especially by Jesus who was able to put the full meaning into it.

Luke 24:36 (NIV) also John 20:19,21 & 26
...Jesus himself stood among them and said to them, "Peace be with you."

It is a wonderful thing that in the plan of God that just as Ishmael was related to Isaac, so the Arabic language is related to the Hebrew language and some of the Arabic customs are related to the Jewish customs including these words of greeting. For the Arabs and Muslims greet in the following way:

Greeting:	*as–Salamu 'alai-kum*	"The peace be on you."
Response:	*Wa 'alai-kum as-Salam*	"And on you also be the peace."

It is therefore very appropriate that we learn this greeting in the Arabic language and that we make full use of it to speak blessing into the homes and lives of those to whom Jesus sends us to minister. This is very fitting since the message we bring is the Gospel of peace (Romans 10:15, KJV) the God we serve is the God of peace (Romans 15:33; 16:20) and His Kingdom is righteousness, **peace** and joy in the Holy Spirit (Romans 14:17). However, we must note that Jesus taught us not to force ourselves upon those who are not ready to welcome us. We should rather leave them, in which case, the peace and blessing of God's presence will depart from them with us as we leave.

The peace that the Christian has in Jesus Christ is unique and unlike anything that the Muslim will experience elsewhere even among his Muslim brothers and sisters.

John 14:27 (NIV)
"Peace I leave with you, peace I give you. I do not give to you as the world gives..."

For as the Bible teaches, Jesus Himself is our peace (Ephesians 2:14). He lives in each Christian through the presence of His Spirit and therefore wherever we go, we take Jesus and His peace with us.

Praying for the Sick and Troubled in Mind and Spirit

Finally, in Jesus' method, he sent his disciples out with authority to heal the sick, raise the dead, cleanse the lepers and drive out demons (Matthew 10:8; Luke 9:2; 10:9). Therefore, wherever we receive a welcome, we should not hesitate to minister in love to those in need. Our experience is that such ministry is often the key that opens the Muslim heart to receive the message of the gospel. This is especially true of Muslims who are living in a foreign land or who have migrated away from their home community. If we know or can see that people are sick or troubled in some way, then we can ask for permission to pray for them there and then. Again in our experience, this is usually accepted as long as it is done with a humble spirit.

Dealing with Fear

We must be careful not to take the analogy of being sheep among wolves too far. A good number of Christians are afraid of Muslims and try to always avoid them due to the age-long notion that they are violent. This is one particular factor that has contributed in no small way to selective witnessing by Christians in the Lord's business.

Not all Muslims are violent or aggressive. There are many who are reasonable and level-headed and do not consider the Islamic religion as a family heritage to be defended at all costs.

In any case, we have not been given the Spirit of fear to scare us from sharing the saving gospel of Christ with our Muslim brothers and sisters.

Psalm 118:6; (NIV)
The Lord is with me; I will not be afraid. What can man do to me?

2 Tim. 1:7
For God hath not given us the spirit of fear, but of power and of love and of a sound mind.

1 Peter 3:13-15 (NIV)
Who is going to harm you if you are eager to do good? But even if you should suffer for what is right you are blessed. "Do not fear what they fear, do not be frightened." But in your hearts set aside Christ as Lord.

Note also that we do not need to fear taking food if it is offered to us for when Jesus sent out his disciples, he said "Eat what is set before you" (Luke 10:8) so let us accept it with thanksgiving.

Our Approach

Mutual Respect

As you share the gospel with Muslims, care must be taken not to hide or compromise with the truth, but in an atmosphere of mutual respect and tolerance. As Peter taught the early Christians, we must always be ready to speak and explain what we believe, but we must do it with gentleness and respect (1 Peter 3:15).

The Qur'an must be viewed with respect as the Muslim views it. It should therefore not be placed on the ground and certainly not trodden on or kicked around. Derogatory remarks about Islam, the Qur'an and the Prophet Muhammad should be avoided. Assuming the witness position without jumping into the judge's seat breeds courtesy, humility and non-confrontation.

One-To-One Approach

Islam is considered as a family and community religion as well as a national religion. Its influence is exerted individually and collectively on the Muslims.

Renouncing one's faith in Islam amounts to renouncing your family, community and nation, hence the difficulty in breaking an age-long traditional linkage. No one Muslim stands as an individual, irrespective of age or status. With this kind of permeating influence, it would be preferable and most effective to engage one Muslim at a time. Group witnessing usually never ends successfully or profitably.

Sensitivity

Due to various reasons, not all Muslims would kindly welcome Christians who would like to witness to them about Christ. In such cases, if one insists on engaging the Muslim, the situation may get out of hand. Preferably, an appointed time could be sought from the Muslim to enable him to overcome any fear on his or her part.

Muslims can best be engaged, only, in an atmosphere of peace, love and mutual respect. Be sensitive to situations.

Gender Barrier

While many modern Muslims do not accept the fact that women are relegated to the background, women continue to be segregated from men in practice; for instance, in the mosque and other gatherings. The gender barrier is reinforced by other practices; for instance, men should not shake hands with women. This makes it highly detestable for a female Christian to engage a male Muslim by sharing the gospel with him. Even a Muslim male would not easily accept his Christian wife to witness to him about Christ. Likewise it is not appropriate for a man on his own to approach a woman on her own.

Points For Discussion

To facilitate decision making at the end of the discussion period, it is more effective to treat one topic at a time rather than jumping from one to another. One must be extra careful and attentive to be able to direct the discussion along the topic at stake. There is the tendency for a Muslim to divert the course of discussion with an irrelevant question. Allow the Muslim enough time to speak, while you listen carefully and attentively in order to correct wrong statements and contribute effectively.

The Use of the Qur'an and the Bible

Just as the fork aids the knife in eating, so does the Qur'an greatly assist in providing convincing answers to most of the questions that come from Muslims and would-be Muslims during evangelism. Yet most Christians are yet to realise this. Some Christians even hold the view that the mere reading of the Qur'an invokes God's displeasure, and even curses. This view, in my opinion, is wrong.

It is common to find Christians who discourage the use of the Qur'an in evangelism. They argue that it is unnecessary since Jesus never used it, it is not God's word and therefore it has no authority. All these points are fine but we do well to observe what the Muslim missionaries and teachers are doing. When they preach in public on the TV or radio, they usually use the Bible. Do you think that they do this because they believe in it as Christians do? No, they are rather using it as a bait to attract unsuspecting Christians and non-Christians alike. They have learned to quote Bible verses very well and pick and choose very cleverly so as to add credence to their false claims and cause confusion. They are making frantic efforts to put Islam and Christianity on the same plane as if Islam were the continuation and perfect form of Christianity.

In contrast, Christians appear to be so helpless as they see how the Muslims are growing in number. When the Christian comes to witness to the Muslim, the Christian discovers how well the Muslim can quote from the Bible and yet the Christian is totally ignorant of the Qur'an and feels completely disarmed. Yet what is there to stop the Christian from acquiring knowledge in the Qur'an and using it to reach Muslims?

One does not have to learn the whole Qur'an but it is useful to memorise at least some of the basic parallel truths which are found in both the Bible and the Qur'an.

It will probably surprise most Christians to realise how much truth is in fact contained in the Qur'an about Jesus Christ and his Lordship over all. (See the arguments used in the companion book "Ishmael shall be blessed" for details). Just as the Jews were taught to follow the Jewish law and traditions without understanding the meaning, so do many Muslims follow certain practices (such as ablutions) without fully understanding why. They then query why Christians do not do the same things. In this situation, the Muslim can better appreciate the Christian's defence when the full significance of such practices are unfolded from the Islamic point of view. In such situations it has been found to be much easier and more convincing to begin with the Qur'an and the Hadith to clear the Muslim's mind of all misconceptions.

Having said all this, every Christian can be encouraged to know that the Muslim respects the Bible and will listen to it. So lack of knowledge of the Qur'an is no excuse for not beginning to witness to our Muslim friends and neighbours. In fact, the Bible is most effective because it is God's word and it has great power when applied by the Holy Spirit. Indeed it is sharper than any two-edged sword.

A Word of Caution

Experience shows that it is better to desist from using the Qur'an if you are not knowledgeable in it. Don't feel pressurised to use it nor decide it is a good idea to use it simply because others are doing so. If you do want to use it, make sure that you know it well and avoid misquotation or misrepresentation. Also make sure that the parts you are quoting relate exactly to the topic at stake. For knowledgeable Muslims will be quick to pounce on your mistakes and use them to discredit you before others.

Islamic Knowledge

Many Christians consider that gaining knowledge in Islam is unnecessary. Yet, such an arrogant attitude has led many Christians into making wrong pronouncements that easily irritate and provoke the Muslim audience into uncontrollable anger, resulting in religious conflicts.

An in-depth knowledge of Islam is a necessary and an indispensable tool, if the "walled Muslim community" is to be penetrated with the power and truth of the gospel that we have at our disposal.

The reader is encouraged to read the following sections of this book well in order to help build up such knowledge.

DOs and DON'Ts

Do talk to one Muslim at a time in personal evangelism.
Do become the Muslim in order to win him or her for Christ (see 1 Corinthians 9:19-23).

1. **Do** show respect to Allah, Muhammad, Islam and the Qur'an.
2. **Don't** begin by saying something that will offend and provoke an argument.
3. **Do** use the Qur'an to gain attention and respect, but **don't** use it as the Word of God.
4. **Do** learn to recite a few verses of the Qur'an in Arabic.
5. **Don't use** the Qur'an if you are not well versed in it.
6. **Do** make sure that the verses you quote are relevant to the topic under discussion.
7. **Don't** witness to a woman alone if you are a man and **don't** witness to man alone if you are a woman.
8. **Don't** ask or allow a woman convert to give her testimony in front of a Muslim audience.
9. **Don't** ask or allow any new Muslim convert to give a testimony in front a Muslim audience.

10. **Don't** use the *Azaan* (the Muslim call to prayer) to call the Muslims to gather so that you can preach to them.
11. **Do** seek to make friends with Muslims and show them love and concern before presenting the gospel to them.

Answers To Muslims' Excuses

1. I cannot change my religion.
   But Muhammad rejected his father's religion and Ghulam Ahmad left the Shi'a sect.

2. I cannot leave friends and relations.
   But parents have no authority over children in such matters and they cannot help you on the Judgement Day.

Qur'an 60:3
Of no profit to you will be your relatives and your children on the day of judgement: He will judge between you: for God sees well all that ye do.

Qur'an 31:33
O mankind! Do your duty to your Lord, and fear (The coming of) a Day when no father can avail aught for his son, nor a son avail aught for his father. Verily, the promise of God is true: let not then this present life deceive you, not let the Chief Deceiver deceive you about God.

Qur'an 2:23
And if ye are in doubt as to what we have revealed from time to time to our servant, then produce a Sura like thereunto; and call your witnesses or helpers (If there are any) besides God, if your (doubts) are true.

Qur'an 80:34-37
That day shall a man flee from his own brother, and from his mother and his father, and from his wife and his children. Each one of them, that day, will have enough concern (of his own) to make him indifferent to the others.

Everyone is responsible for his own deeds.

Qur'an 10:41
If they charge thee with falsehood, say: "My work to me, and yours to you! Ye are free from responsibility for what I do, and I for what ye do!

3.   Muhammad can lead me to heaven.

Are you sure? You are rather required to pray for him!

Qur'an 33:56
God and His Angels send blessings on the Prophet: O ye that believe! Send ye blessings on him, and salute him with all respect."

Muhammad himself had to ask for the way.

Qur'an 1:6
Show us the Straight Way.

He is not sure of his own fate, so how can he be sure of yours?

Qur'an 46:9
Say: "I am no bringer of newfangled doctrine among the apostles, nor do I know what will be done with me or with you. I follow but that which is revealed to me by inspiration; I am but a Warner open and clear."

The blind cannot lead the blind.

4.   I don't need Jesus.
Everyone is a sinner except Jesus.

Qur'an 16:61
If God were to punish men for their wrong-doing, he would not leave, on the (earth), a single living creature: But He gives them respite for a stated term: when their term expires, they would not be able to delay (the punishment) for a single hour, just as they would not be able to anticipate it (for a single hour).

He alone deals with sin.

Qur'an 3:39
While he was standing in prayer in the chamber, the angels called unto him: "God doth give thee glad tidings of Yahya, witnessing the truth of a word from God, and (be besides) noble, chaste, and a Prophet, of the (goodly) company of the righteous."

5.   I will be persecuted.
You may be, but God will enable you to endure and will bless and reward you.

Matthew 5:11,12
Blessed are ye, when men shall revile you, and persecute you, and shall say all manner of evil against you falsely, for my sake. Rejoice, and be exceeding glad: for great is your reward in heaven: for so persecuted they the prophets which were before you.

2 Timothy 3:12
Yea, and all that will live godly life in Christ Jesus shall suffer persecution.

Revelation 2:10
Fear none of those things which thou shalt suffer: behold, the devil shall cast some of you into prison, that ye may be tried; and ye shall have tribulation ten days: be thou faithful unto death, and I will give thee a crown of life."

6. **But I believe in Jesus as all Muslims do.**
Jesus is more than a Prophet.

Qur'an 4:171
...Christ Jesus the son of Mary was (no more than) an apostle of Allah, and His Word, which He bestowed on Mary, and a Spirit proceeding from Him: so believe in Allah and His apostles...

John's (Yahya's) testimony.

Qur'an 3:39
*While he was standing in prayer in the chamber, the angels called unto him: "God doeth give thee glad tidings of Yahya, witnessing the truth of a **Word from God**, and (be besides) noble, chaste, and a Prophet – of the (goodly) company of the righteous.*

John 1:29
The next day John saw Jesus coming unto him, and said, "Behold, the Lamb of God, who taketh away the sin of the world!"

The angels' testimony.

Qur'an 3:45
*Behold! The angels said: "O Mary! God giveth thee glad tidings of a **Word** From Him: his name will be Christ Jesus, the son of Mary, held in honour in this world and the hereafter and of (the company of) those nearest to God;"*

The Bible requires us to make a clear confession about Jesus:

Romans 10:9 (NIV)
If you confess with your mouth, "Jesus is Lord" and believe in your heart that God raised him from the dead, you will be saved.

5

UNDERSTANDING ISLAM

The Origin And Meaning Of Islam

The word Islam is derived from the Arabic root *SLM* which means, among other things, peace, purity, submission and obedience. Muhammad was the founder of the religion and therefore it was earlier known as Muhammadanism. However, Muhammad himself called it *Islam* and this is the name used by its adherents. Muslims reject the words "Muhammadanism" and "Muhammadans" as describing their religion and its adherents. To them, their religion does not take its name after a mortal being, neither do they worship Muhammad or believe in him in the same way as Christians believe in Jesus.

They do not even accept that their religion was "founded" by Muhammad. Muhammad was only a mortal being commissioned by Allah to teach Allah's way to mankind. Allah stands alone in history as the Creator and the One who is to be worshipped, while Muhammad is His Messenger. The Muslim worships Allah (God) alone and he regards Allah as the original founder of Islam, which dates back to the age of Adam.

Muslims do however, greatly respect Muhammad and refer to him in such terms as "The Holy Prophet of Islam" or "Allah's Noble Prophet." Whenever they mention his name they add the words *Sallallahu 'Alaihi Wasallam* (abbreviated in writing as S.A.W.) which is translated in English as "Peace be upon Him" (abbreviated in writing as P.B.U.H.).

Any human being who submits to and obeys Allah (God) is a Muslim according to Islam. It is in this sense that the Qur'an calls Abraham and the other biblical prophets Muslims. So in the Qur'anic context, it is not just the followers of Muhammad who are Muslims, but anyone who follows Abraham, Moses, Jesus and the rest of God's messengers.

It is worth noting here that, although the Qur'an refers to all prophets as Muslims, it shows how in their life-time each one failed to submit fully to God. At some point in their life, they submitted to Satan and sinned and hence they were required by God to ask for forgiveness of sins. This is quite logical because submission to Satan is not Islam. Islam refers to submission to God only. Jesus Christ, who never sinned against God and therefore needed no forgiveness from God, stands out unique among the whole of God's prophets. He is above all prophets and superior to them all. Hence his unique title, *Ruhu'llah* – the Spirit of God. Consistent with this, the Qur'an confirms that Jesus was holy (Q.19:19).

In contrast, Muhammad was asked to pray for the forgiveness of his sins in several places of the Qur'an (Q. 48:2; 47:19).

(For discussion on this issue see "In whom can true Islam be found" in the companion book "Ishmael shall be blessed").

The Muslim seeks to worship and submit himself to Allah and calls on Allah to help him in this task:

Qur'an 1:2-7
Praise be to Allah,
The Cherisher and Sustainer of the Worlds;
Most Gracious, Most Merciful;
Master of the Day of Judgment.
Thee do we worship, and Thine aid we seek.
Show us the straight way,
The way of those on whom Thou hast bestowed Thy Grace,
Those whose (portion) is not wrath, and who go not astray.

The Qur'an is Allah's Revelation, which was given through Muhammad, as guidance to enable the Muslim to walk in the way of Islam (submission to God).

Muhammad and the Establishment of Islam

Muhammad's Birth and Childhood

A town in the Arabian peninsular known as Mecca has been celebrated through the ages as the location of the "Holy House of God" (*Ka'batullah*) – an ancient monument sacred to the Arabs. By the sixth century of the Christian Era, it was a very busy commercial centre under the control of an Arab tribe called the Quraysh which had settled in and around Mecca. The custodian of the Ka'ba at that time was Abdu'l Muttalib, the head of the Hashim family. His son, Abdullah, married a woman from Yathrib (Medina) called Aminah and it was they who gave birth to Muhammad.

The birth was notable in that it took place during the Year of the Elephant –AD 570 so-called because in that year an army marched towards Mecca with a huge elephant. They were led by Abrahatu 'l-Ashram an Abyssian Christian who was the Viceroy of the king of Saana in Saba (Yemen). Their intention was to use the elephant to demolish the Ka'ba, which was known as a centre of paganism. However, the people of Mecca offered up prayers and during the night the army was suddenly struck down with a plague that caused many deaths. The natural explanation would be that it was smallpox, but the Meccans reported that the gods had sent a flock of birds to throw stones on the soldiers who then developed sores and pustules. Muhammad later attributed this miraculous deliverance to Allah alone (Sura 105).

When she was six months pregnant, Aminah's husband, Abdullah, fell ill and died on his return from a trading expedition to Syria. It was thus 'Abdu'l Muttalib who took the responsibility to name his grandson. He carried him in his arms to the Ka'ba and there he named him "Muhammad" which literally means "Praised One." Muhammad is sometimes spelt as Mohammed, Mohomed, or Mohomet.

Muhammad was first nursed by a slave-girl called Suwaibah as the Arabian custom demanded and then later, another woman called Halimah looked after him. One day, when Muhammad was out with his foster brother, two men clothed in white garments took hold of him, threw him on the ground, ripped open his belly and began stirring it up. At this, the foster-brother ran to his parents and told them what was happening. They rushed to the place where Muhammad was, but found him standing erect and in one piece, although looking very pale. They asked him, "what has happened to thee child?" and he answered "Two men came and threw me down and ripped open my belly." He added that he did not know what they were looking for in there.

Then Halimah's husband said, "I greatly fear that the boy has got epilepsy." So Halimah took him back to his mother Aminah. Halimah said to her "I am afraid that he is possessed by a devil." But Aminah responded, "what in the world can Satan have to do with my son that he should be his enemy?" and then she spoke of the wonderful circumstances surrounding his birth.

In his sixth year, Muhammad was taken by his mother on a journey to Medina but on return his mother died. His grandfather 'Abdu'l-Muttalib, who then took charge of him, died just two years later and so then he was committed to the care of his paternal uncle, Abu Talib. At the age of 12, Muhammad was taken on a mercantile journey to Syria and Busra for some months.

According to Muslim historian, Abu'l-Fida, it was at Syria that Muhammad was brought into contact with the profession of Christianity. He then had the opportunity of obtaining some information as to the national and social customs of Christians. It is therefore, highly probable that it was at this time that Muhammad's mind became first impressed with the absolute necessity of reforming, not only the gross idolatry of Mecca, but the degrading social habits of the Arabian people.

After this journey, history is mostly silent concerning the youth of Muhammad. But Muhammad, though a lad, was said to have accompanied his uncle, on the sacrilegious war which broke out between the Quraysh and the Banu Hawazin between the years AD 580-590.

Muhammad's Early Married Life

When Muhammad was twenty-five, he entered into the service of Khadijah, a rich widow of Mecca. Muhammad was placed in charge of the widow's merchandise and had the chance of repeating a mercantile journey on the same route he had trodden with his uncle 13 years ago. He visited Aleppo and Damascus and undoubtedly was brought into frequent contact with the Jews and Christians. He had another chance of obtaining an acquaintance with the Jewish and Christian faiths. This enabled him to embody so much of the teaching of the Bible in the verses of the Qur'an.

Muhammad, proving himself faithful in her mistress' business, was rewarded with Khadijah's hand in marriage. At that time she was forty years of age and their marriage was blessed with two sons and four daughters. Unfortunately, the two sons, al-Qasim and 'Abdu'llah died leaving the four daughters Zainab, Ruqaiyah, Ummu Kulsum and Fatimah.

During her lifetime, Khadijah was Muhammad's only wife. Muhammad as at this time was still unknown to the outside world. He gained a reputation when he took a prominent part in the resuscitation of an old league called the Federation of the Fuzul. At the age of 35, as he was entering the Ka'ba one day, he was called upon to act as referee on which tribe should have the honour of repositioning the "Black Stone" during the rebuilding of the Ka'ba. The situation had become so tense it seemed that war was about to break out. Muhammad wisely suggested that the Black Stone be placed on a cloth so that representatives from all the tribes could lift the stone together. With this solution the builders were able to continue their work and complete the reconstruction.

The Revelations Begin

When he was about forty years of age his mind became perplexed with trying to find the true religion. He was greatly troubled by the idolatry and moral debasement of his people but at the same time the teaching he had received about Judaism and Christianity was very confused and he had a lot of doubts.

According to Ayisha, the first revelations that the Prophet of Allah received were in true dreams. He was in the habit of retiring to the seclusion of a cave in Mount Hira in order to pray and meditate. One night, as he was sleeping, he was visited by an angel who was holding a silk brocade with words written on it. The angel commanded him to read or recite the words on the brocade and squeezed him in persuasion. He did this twice and both times, Muhammad pleaded "I am not a reader." However, the angel gave the order a third time and increased the pressure on Muhammad.

Eventually, albeit with a trembling heart, Muhammad managed to repeat the words after the angel. When he awoke, the words were imprinted on his heart and he was troubled greatly, fearing that he had become possessed.

He arrived back in Mecca trembling with fear and cried out "Wrap me up! Wrap me up!" He remained wrapped in the garment until his fear was dispelled and he was able to tell Khadijah what had happened. He told her, "I was afraid I should die." Then Khadijah consoled him and said, "No, it will not be so I swear by Allah..." After this, she took the Prophet to Waraqah, her uncle's son. When she had explained the reason for their visit, Waraqah asked Muhammad, "O, son of my uncle, what did you see?" When Muhammad had told him, Waraqah declared, "This is the Nemus," meaning that this was the same angel, spirit or being that God had sent to Moses.

There followed a considerable period during which Muhammad received no further revelation but rather experienced a period of darkness. During this time he suffered so many doubts and so much mental depression that he wished to throw himself from the top of a hill and destroy himself. However, after some time, while he lay stretched out on his carpet and wrapped up in his garments, the angel is said to have returned with further revelations. He hailed Muhammad as the "Apostle of Allah" and commanded him to proclaim publicly what had been revealed to him. Muhammad then believed himself to be a commissioned Apostle, the messenger and the prophet of Allah, sent to reclaim a fallen people to the knowledge and service of their God. His revelations were Allah's Book and his sayings the utterances of inspiration.

Islam Founded as a Religion

The first convert to Islam was his faithful wife Khadijah, the next two, Ali and Zaid, his adopted children, and afterwards his old trusted friend Abu Bakr, "The true". Then followed 'Usman who was a grandson of 'Abdu 'l-Muttalib; Talhah, the renamed warrior of after days; and 'Abdu'r-Rahman, a merchant. The new converts soon numbered some fifty souls. They were either members of the Prophet's family or his dearest friends. As the number of the converts grew so did hostility from the rest of the people of Mecca. In order to escape danger, Muhammad urged eleven of his men with their families to flee and seek asylum in Abyssinia (present-day Ethiopia). Muhammad knew that the people there were Christians and indeed the emigrants were met with the kind reception of Negus, the king and his people who allowed them to live in peace and comfort. This is known as the first *Hijrah* or "flight." They returned to Mecca after about three months.

Around this same time, Muhammad sought a compromise with the Meccans, by admitting gods into his system as intercessors with the Supreme God, Allah. He brought the following Sura to them as they were sitting at the Ka'ba:

And see ye not Lat and Uzza, and Manat the third besides? These are exalted females and verily their intercession is to be hoped for.

But afterwards Muhammad's mind was not at ease and it was not long before the angel returned to him and recalled the latter part of this verse saying that it had been brought by Satan. Instead he revealed an uncompromising statement against idolatry which is in the Qur'an as we find it today:

Qur'an 53: 19-25
Have ye seen Lat, and Uzza, and another, the third (goddess), Manat? What! For you the male sex, and for Him, the female? Behold, such would be indeed a division most unfair! These are nothing but names which ye have devised, --ye and your fathers, --for which Allah has sent down no authority (whatever). They follow nothing but conjecture and what their own souls desire! --even though there has already come to them Guidance from their Lord! Nay, shall man have (just) anything he hankers after? But it is to Allah that the End and the Beginning (of all things) belong.

In the sixth year of his mission, the cause of Muhammad was strengthened by two powerful citizens, Hamzah and 'Umar who joined his cause. However, this caused the other Meccans to feel even more threatened and therefore brought further conflict between them and Muhammad and his followers.

In the beginning of the tenth year of his mission, and in the fiftieth year of his life, Muhammad lost his wife, Kadijah, who was then 65 years old. For twenty-five years, she had been his counsellor and support and his grief at her death at first was inconsolable. Abu Talib, the prophet's uncle and guardian also died two weeks after Khadijah's death. His conversion to Islam is a matter of uncertainty. Within two months of his wife's death, Muhammad married Saudah, the widow of one of the Abyssinian emigrants and also betrothed himself to Ayisha, the daughter of his friend Abu Bakr. She was then just a girl of seven years.

An attempt to preach his new religion at Ta'if, resulted in him being hooted at and pelted with stone, and his message still only met with hostility in Mecca. However, there was a change in his fortunes when some Yathribites, who he met during the annual pilgrimage to the Ka'ba, entered into a pact with Muhammad and invited him to be their leader in order to help resolve the differences between them. A teacher was sent back with them and by the time of the next pilgrimage, Muhammad discovered that he had 70 willing disciples in Yathrib. They also entered into a pact with him and vowed to defend him at the cost of their lives. So from that time, Muhammad determined to move his base to Yathrib. He sent his Meccan disciples ahead in small groups secretly until only he, Abu Bakr and Ali remained with their families. The emigrants, who numbered around 150, became known as the *Muhajirun* - "Refugees," whereas those who received them at Medina are known as the *Ansah* - "allies" or "assistants."

At this time the Quraysh held a council and decided that Muhammad should be killed. However, before they could act, someone was able to warn him and he escaped to Mount Saur where he hid for three days before continuing a further three days into Yathrib.

The Muhammadan Era Begins

The day of his flight - the *Hijrah* (calculated as 20 June, AD 622) marks the beginning of the Muhammadan era or Hegira from which the Islamic calendar is dated. (Years are thus reported as AH rather than AD).

During his first year in Yathrib, he was mainly occupied with building the great mosque and providing houses for himself and his followers. He moved Saudah into her own residence and then consummated his marriage with Ayisha who was still a child at just ten years old. Thus at the age of fifty-three, a new phase commenced in the life of Muhammad. He surrendered himself to the cares and discord of polygamy and the unity of his family was broken, never again to be restored.

In a short time he became recognised as the chief of Yathrib and his political rule was established. He renamed the city *al-Madinah* (Medina) which means "the city." From this time there was a change in the character of the portions of the Qur'an that were revealed to Muhammad. At Mecca he was presented as the admonisher and persuader, but in Medina he became the legislator and warrior and the verses of the Qur'an become more directive with prose replacing poetry. Muhammad openly assumed the office of "Warner" and prophet.

The Islamic Jihad Begins

During his second year in Medina, Muhammad commenced hostilities against the Quraysh and the first battle took place at Badr. Muhammad encouraged his army of 350 followers with the promise that Allah would assist them and that if anyone should fall in the battle, he would go straight to Paradise. The Quraysh mustered an army three times larger than Muhammad's. However, there was some dissent among them as to whether it was right to fight against their fellow tribesmen or not and once the battle began, Muhammad's forces were able to rout them.

Muhammad was received in triumph in Medina on his return from the battle, but his joy was interrupted with the death of his daughter Ruqaiyah. Muhammad's position was now greatly strengthened and from this point onwards, the Qur'an assumed a "rude, dictatorial tone" (Hughes pg. 376).

The Jews however, remained unimpressed and were slow to acknowledge Muhammad, even though he claimed to be the teacher of the creed of Abraham. Muhammad therefore sought for a plausible excuse to severe any relationship with them. The opportunity soon arose when a Muslim girl was insulted by a youth of a Jewish tribe. The whole tribe was attacked and forced out of Medina and their houses and lands were confiscated and divided amongst the followers of Muhammad. Around this time Muhammad married his fourth wife, Hafsah, the daughter of Umar.

Meanwhile, the tidings of the defeat at Badr had aroused the bitterest feelings among the Quraysh. They advanced towards Medina with an army of 3,000 strong men. Muhammad led out his force of 1,000 men and after camping overnight led the attack on the enemy camp. However, they were abandoned by 300 men under the leadership of Abdullah, chief of the "Hypocrites" (citizens of Medina who because of political expediency had only pretended to embrace Islam). Thus the remainder of the Muslim army was left to face the Quraysh who were not slow in their counter-attack. The Quraysh raised the cry, "Muhammad is slain!" bringing utter confusion in the Muslim ranks and thus Muhammad and his followers fled in defeat. Having made their point the Quraysh did not attempt to pursue them.

From this time on, Muslim forces were sent out on a number of military expeditions against various Jewish and Arab tribes. A second expedition was also made to Badr but the Quraysh refused to fight and Muhammad counted it as a triumph. On returning to Medina, Muhammad married the widow 'Ubaidah, whose husband had fallen at Badr, as his fifth wife, and Ummu Salimah, the widow of Abu Salimah, who fell at the battle of Uhud, for his sixth. By these two additions to his harem, he exceeded the legal number of four wives to which he restricted his followers. At some point he also married Ummu Habibah, the widow of Ubaidu'llah, a Muslim who emigrated to Abyssinia and became and remained a Christian until his death.

In another expedition the Muslim army besieged the Jewish tribe known as the Banu Quraizah. They endured for 25 days but were then forced to submit to the Muslims. Their fate was left to the decision of Sa'd, a companion of the Prophet. He decreed that all the male Jews should be executed and the females and their children taken as slaves. The Prophet commended this wicked sentence as being the judgement of Allah (Qur'an 33:26) and 700 men were beheaded. Muhammad reserved one of the Jewish female captives, Rihanah, for himself to be his concubine.

Also, before the close of that same year, Muhammad married his cousin Zainab. The Prophet had previously given her in marriage to Zaid Ibn Harisah, his freed man and adopted son. But upon visiting Zaid's house to meet his absence, the Prophet cast his eyes on Zainab and was so smitten with her beauty, that he exclaimed, "Praise belongeth unto Allah, who turneth the hearts of men even as He will." On the return of Zaid, his wife reported that she had made an impression on the Prophet's heart and so

Zaid offered to divorce her in preference to his friend and benefactor. However, the relations of Arabs to their adopted children were so strict, that nothing short of a divine revelation could settle the matter. Thus, the Prophet (in the name of Allah and His Apostle) produced the Qur'anic verses Sura 33:36-38 in order to sanction his heart's desire.

After another battle, Muhammad paid for the release of one of the female captives, Juwairiyah, and took her as his eighth wife. Around AD 628 (AH 6), Muhammad conceived the idea that he should write to all the kings, emperors and princes and appeal to them to embrace Islam. Some tore up the letter in anger while others felt honoured by it. Jarih ibn Matta al Muqauqis the governor of Egypt sent two Coptic (Christian) slave girls to Muhammad to show his appreciation. Muhammad gave one away and kept the other who was named Mariyah (Mary) as his second concubine. In due time she was able to present a son to him, who was named Ibrahim. One day Hafsah caught Muhammad in her room with Mariyah on the day he was due to be with Ayisha. Although Muhammad begged her to keep it secret, she told Ayisha causing much dissent. Muhammad counted it as a conspiracy against him, but because her father Umar had become very powerful, Hafsah was able to intimidate Muhammad. His only way to solve the problem was to bring another "revelation" which condemned the conspirators and threatened them with divorce, (Qur'an 66:1-5).

Again Muhammad and his followers marched against Khaibar, a fertile district inhabited by Jews and conquered and took captives. Amongst the captives was Safiyah, the widow of the chief of the Jews who had been killed. One of Muhammad's followers begged her for himself, but the Prophet struck with her beauty, threw his mantle over her, and took her to his harem. It was during the

Khaibar expedition that Muhammad instituted Mut'ah, an abominable temporary marriage, which allowed the members of his army to satisfy their carnal desires while away from their wives.

Muhammad marched with his faithful to Makkali where he negotiated an alliance with Maimunah, his eleventh and last wife. His marriage gained him two most important converts, Khalid and 'Amr, who were to carry the standards of Islam to foreign lands.

Finally, on 1st January AD 630, Muhammad began his march to take the city of Mecca. By the time he arrived there, his army had swelled to 10,000 and the Meccans had no choice but to surrender and allow him to enter the city. When he entered the Ka'ba, he saw several pictures of angels and ordered their removal while he shouted "*Allahu Akbar! Allahu Akbar!*" He also ordered the destruction of all 360 idols. Having thus cleansed the Ka'ba, he decreed that from that time forth it would be the *Qibla* to which all Muslims must direct their prayers. After two weeks he left to continue his military campaigns through which the whole of Arabia came under submission to his political and spiritual leadership.

In all, Muhammad had a total of eleven "pure" wives and two concubines. He became very jealous of his wives and as a result produced a divine command that forbade them to re-marry after his death. He had seven children of which six were given birth to by Khadijah and the one surviving boy, Ibrahim, by Mariyah.

The Farewell Pilgrimage -Hijjatu Al-Wadda'a (AD 632)

In March 632, Muhammad led in person the greater pilgrimage to Mecca; the Hajj. It was the first time he had done so, for Abu-Bakr had been the leader in the previous year. The Pilgrimage was now a purely Muslim rite since idolaters were forbidden to attend. The pilgrimage of 632 came to be regarded as establishing the course and form of the ceremonies in general outline that have been followed since. It was also the occasion when the Prophet received the revelation of the last verses of the Qur'an. It concludes:

Qur'an 5:4

...This day have those who reject faith given up all hope of your religion: Yet fear them not but fear Me. This day have I perfected your religion for you, completed my favour upon you, and have chosen for you Islam as your religion... But if any if forced by hunger, with no inclination to transgression, God is indeed Oft-forgiving, most merciful.

By this revelation, it seemed that the mission of the Prophet was complete.

On the eleventh day of Dhu-Hijja the Prophet stood before a large gathering of Muslim pilgrims in the valley of Muzadlifah and delivered a sermon framed in Islamic history as the "Farewell Sermon" of the Prophet. This Pilgrimage is also known as the "Farewell Pilgrimage" because the Prophet did not get the opportunity to meet the Muslims at a pilgrimage again but died only about three months later.

The Prophet began his sermon with praises and glorification of Allah. He addressed the assembled pilgrims in the following words:-

1. "O men lend me your attentive ears. For I do not know whether I will stand before you again in this valley and address you as I address today. Just as you regard this month as sacred, so has Allah made your lives and

possessions inviolate to attacks by one another until the judgement day. Allah has appointed for everyone a share of inheritance. No 'will' shall now be admitted which is prejudicial to the interest of the rightful heir, a child of the father in that house. Whoever contests the parentage of this child will be liable to punishment under the law of Islam. If anyone attributes his birth to someone else's father or falsely claims someone to be his master, Allah, His angels and the whole mankind will curse him. Return goods entrusted to you to their rightful owners. Satan has despaired of leading you astray in big things so beware of obeying him in small things."

2. "O men you have some rights over your wives and your wives also have some rights over you. Your rights against them is that they should live chaste lives and not adopt ways which may bring disgrace to the husband in the sight of his people. If your wives do not live up to this, then punish them after due enquiry has been made by a competent authority and your right to punish has been established. Even punishment in such a case should not be very severe. Always treat your wives well. Allah charged you with looking after them. Women are frail and cannot even protect their own rights. When you married, Allah appointed you the trustees of those rights. You brought your wives to your homes under the injunctions of Allah. You must not therefore abuse such trust which Allah has placed in your hands."

3. "O people you still have in possession prisoners of war. I advise you to feed them and clothe them in the same way you feed and clothe yourselves ..."

4. "Hearken! Worship your Lord, say your prayers fast in the month of Ramadan; and give your wealth in charity. All Muslims, free or enslaved have the same

rights and responsibilities. None is higher than the other unless he is higher in righteousness…"

5. "I have left with you something which, if you will hold fast to, you will never fall into error, - the Book of Allah (Qur'an) and the practice of His Prophet (Sunnah); so give good heed to what I say."

6. Know that every Muslim is a brother, and that Muslims are brethren. It is only lawful to take from a brother what he gives you willingly; so wrong not yourselves."

In conclusion he said: "What I have told you, communicate to the ends of the earth. Maybe those who had not heard may benefit more than those who have heard."

Having said this, the Prophet turned his face up to the heavens and said: "O Allah! Be my witness that I have conveyed Thy message to the people."

The Last Days of the Prophet Muhammad.

Having returned from the pilgrimage, the Prophet had wind of the Byzantine army's preparations against Islam. He then began to prepare an army under Usama B. Zayd to send to the Syrian border. During the preparations, which took place before the end of Safar at the beginning of Rabi ul-Awwal, he went to the public graveyard called Baq'ul Charqad in the middle of the night and prayed for the dead. It was on returning to his family in the morning that he took ill and his suffering began.

For some days he continued to visit the mosque and led the congregational prayers. Then he became too weak to do this. One day he addressed the Muslims in the mosque saying: "Allah offered to elect one from among His servants, the choice of this earth or that which came nigh unto Him and he has chosen that which is nigh unto Allah."

Abu Bakr, who understood the sayings of the Prophet best realised that the end of the Prophet was nigh. With tears rolling down his cheeks, he said "We would rather sacrifice our lives and those of our parents."

The Prophet also appointed Abu Bakr to lead the congregation in prayers and commanded all doors leading to the Mosque to be kept shut save that of Abu Bakr. These were a clear indication that Abu Bakr was to succeed him even though the prophet made no mention of that explicitly.

When his condition became worse, he sought the permission of all his wives to be attended to in Ayisha's room.

Due to the seriousness of his illness the army of Usama encamped at Al-Jurf, about a stage from Medina, to see what Allah would decide about the Apostle.

The Prophet ordered the Muhajirun to be kind to the Ansar. He warned Muslims against taking his tomb for a place of worship. He would also say "Woe to the Jews and the Christians for they have taken the tombs of their Prophets for places of worship (Masjid)." He again said "Do not exalt me as the Christian have exalted the son of Mary. For, I am a servant of Allah, so call me "Abdu'llah" ("Servant of Allah"). He emphasised several times that Muslims should only worship Allah, the one and only God.

The Prophet Muhammad passed away with the heat of the sun and complaining of severe headache on Monday, 8 June AD 632 in Medina. His head was resting on the bosom of his favourite wife, Ayisha, when he died. According to some other reports, the prophet died of fever. He was 62.

Hujrah

Hujrah means "chamber" and refers to the place where Muhammad died and was buried. It was originally the apartment allotted to Ayisha, Muhammad's favourite wife. It is behind the Prophet's Mosque, at Medina.

Within the building are the tombs of Muhammad, Abu Bakr and Umar, with a space reserved for the grave of our Lord Jesus Christ, whom Muslims say will again visit the earth and die and be in a separate part of the building, although some views differ. Captain Burton gives the annexed plan of the building as below: (Hughes, pg. 183).

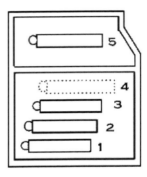

1. Muhammad
2. Abu Bakr
3. Umar
4. The space for the tomb of Jesus
5. Fatimah

The Khalifahs-Successors

The Khalifah is a title given to a successor of Muhammad. He is vested with absolute authority in all matters of state, both civil and religious, as long as he rules in conformity with the law of the Qur'an and the Hadith.

Muhammad (AD 610 – 632)

1. **Abu Bakr** (AD 632 – 634)
   Original name – Abul Kdah; the Prophet changed it to Abdullah. Earned the title As-Siddiq, the "Veracious."

2. **Umar Ibn Al-Kahtab** (AD 632 – 644)
   Reigned for ten years of prosperity after which "Fires", a Persian slave, assassinated him. Initially a fierce

opponent of Muhammad but later he accepted Islam and became a staunch supporter.

3. **Usman Ibn Affan** (AD 644 – 656)
He was assassinated at the age of eighty-two by Muhammad, son of Abu Bakr. He married two daughters of the Prophet, Ruqaiya and Umma Kulsum and was therefore called, "The Possessor of Two Lights."

4. **Ali** (AD 656 – 661)
Assassinated with a poisoned sword by Ibu Muljam at Al-Kufah and died after three days, at the age of 59 years. He married Fatimah, the daughter of the Prophet and had three sons Hassan, Hussain and Muhassin.
The Shi'a hold the view that on the death of Muhammad, Ali was entitled to the Khalifate instead of the first three. This resulted in the formation of the Shi'a sect who held that the Khalifate was to be hereditary from the descendants of Muhammad through Fatimah and Ali. This was in opposition to the Sunni sect which held the view that the Khalifah was to be by election. The above four immediate successors of Muhammad took the title the *Khula faaur – Raashiduum* ("the well directed Khalifahs").

5. **Hassan** (AD 661) Son of Ali, was poisoned and died.

6. **Hussain** (Hassan's brother invited from Medina).
When Hussain was on his way to Kufa, a fierce battle was fought between the house of Mu'awiyah and Hussain's followers at Karbala. Hussain and his son Zaid were killed and the Khalifate passed to the Umayyads (Banu Umayah).

After the Assassination of Ali in AD 661, a great struggle began between the followers of Ali, (the Shi'a) and the house of Mu'awiyah (Sunni) over who should be head of state. Mu'awiyah who had been appointed governor of Syria by his uncle, Usman, held Ali responsible for his uncle's murder. After Ali deposed him he fought back and finally grasped Egypt from Ali and the Khaliphate from both Ali and his sons. During this period, Muslim theology was based on what the first three Khalifahs promulgated. Ali and his descendants, who were known as the Fatimids, were ignored. The Ummayad Dynasty, which ruled from Damascus between 661 – 750, had fourteen Khalifahs.

The Ummayad Dynasty

1.	**Mu'awiyah (I)**	AD	661	Siege of Constantinopole, made Damascus capital.
2.	**Yazid (I)**	AD	679	Destruction of Hussain's party and his death
3.	**Mu'awiyah (II)**			Deposed
4.	**Marwaan (I)**	AD	683	Poisoned
5.	**Abdul Malik**	AD	684	Arabian money first minted
6.	**Al Walid (I)**	AD	705	Conquest of Africa, Spain and Bukhaarah
7.	**Sulaiman**	AD	715	Defeated before Constanstinopole, died of grief
8.	**Umar**	AD	717	Poisoned
9.	**Yazid (II)**	AD	720	

10. Hishaam	AD	724	The rise of the Abbasids
11. Al-Walid (II)			Slain by conspirators
12. Yazid (III)	AD	744	Died of the plague
13. Ibrahim	AD	744	Deposed
14. Maran	AD	744	Defeated by the Abbasids, pursued to Egypt and slain on the bank of the Nile

The death of Maran in AD 749 marked the end of the Ummayah Dynasty and resulted from another great struggle among the Sunnis when the descendants of Abbas, (one of Muhammad's uncles) overthrew the Ummayads and assumed the Khalifate.

This started the second dynasty of Khalifahs known as the **Abbasid** Khalifahs. They were 37 in number and ruled from Baghdad between AD 750–1258. The first was **Abu Abbas As-Saffah,** who ruled from AD 750–754 and the last was **Al-Mustaaim** (from 1240).

Unlike the Ummayads who were approachable, the Abbasids ruled more like monarchs and surrounded themselves with many officials who needed to be bribed before a hearing could be obtained. They included some of the most tyrannical leaders the world has ever known. The height of their power was marked by great economic prosperity, and notable developments in the arts, sciences and agriculture. However this was short-lived and the unity of the empire began to crumble as Persia, Spain, Morocco, Tunisia and Egypt all broke away under their own rulers. Finally, Hülagü Khan, the grandson of the infamous Mongolian emperor, Genghis Khan, invaded Baghdad and killed the last of its rulers in 1258. The Khalifate continued but was stripped of all political power.

Islam had spread far and wide from Spain to China. Four dynasties ruled in Spain:

1.	Ummayads	AD	855-1057
2.	Mulasamins	AD	1057-1120
3.	Musahidins	AD	1120-1231
4.	The Moors	AD	1251-1473

Two dynasties ruled in Egypt.

1.	Fatimids	AD	787-1172	fourteen Khalifahs
2.	Abbasids	AD	1250-1473	

Finally the Khaliphate passed on to the Turks in 1517, and came to an end when the last Khalifah of the Sunnis, Abdul Hamid, was deposed in 1876.

The Islamic Beliefs – The Articles of Faith

The Islamic beliefs are commonly referred to as the "Articles of Faith." Every Muslim believes in:

1. **The Oneness of God (Tawheed).**
   There is no other god apart from *Allah* (God). Allah is the one who created the heavens and the earth and only Allah is worthy of worship.
   With this belief, Muslims entirely refute the Christian doctrine of the Trinity, which the Qur'an wrongly represents as the three different personalities of the Father, the Son and the Mother.

Q. 5:117
And behold! Allah will say: "O Jesus the son of Mary! Didst thou say unto men, 'Worship me and my mother as gods in derogation of Allah'?" He will say: "Glory to Thee! Never could I say what I had no right (to say). Had I said such a thing, Thou wouldst indeed have known it.

Note that: *Allah* is the only word for God in the Arabic language and is derived from the same Semitic root word (meaning "power") as *El* the Hebrew word for God.

There are 99 "beautiful" names that are given to Allah which describe his qualities such as "The Merciful"

2.   The Prophets.

All the messengers (prophets) of God should be viewed equally without any discrimination. To them, every known nation had a "Warner" or messenger from God. The Qur'an mentions the names of twenty-five of them. With the exception of Muhammad, they were known as national or local messengers, but their message and religion were basically the same and could equally be called **Islam**. Among them, Muhammad stands as the last messenger. Some of the great prophets include Noah, Abraham, Ishmael, Moses, Jesus and Muhammad.

3.   The Qur'an.

To the Muslims, the only authentic and complete book of God in existence today is the *Qur'an* that was given to Muhammad.

In the Qur'an, a special reference is made to the books given to:

Moses: *Taurat*   The Law (*Torah*)
David: *Zabur*   The Psalms
Jesus: *Injil*   The Gospel

But Muslims believe that long before the revelation of the Qur'an, some of the scriptures and revelations that they contained had been lost or corrupted while others were forgotten, neglected or concealed. They ask, "Where are the complete and original versions?" To which we can reply, "Do the Muslims have the original Qur'an that existed before Uthman made his standardisation?"

In principle, the Muslim believes in the previous books and revelations; but to the Muslim, the Qur'an is the standard by which all other books are judged; and whatever differs from the Qur'an is either rejected or suspended.

(Refer to "The Qur'an in the Light of the Bible" in the companion book "Ishmael shall be blessed!")

4.   **The Angels of God.**
There are many angels and each is charged with a certain duty. Among them are:

Israil	The Angel of death
Ismail	The angel who accompanied Gabriel in his last visit to the prophet on his sick bed.
Israfil	The Archangel who will sound the trumpet on the Day of Resurrection.
Jabil	The Angel of the Mountains.
Mikail (Michael)	The Archangel

Munkar & Nakir	The angels who visit the dead in their graves and interrogate them about the prophet Muhammad and Islam.
Jibril (Gabriel)	The Angel of Glad Tidings.
Jinns	Spiritual beings somewhere between angels and human beings. Can be good or evil, but usually thought of as evil. Will come under the same judgement as people.
Iblis (Satan)	The Devil who is the leader of the Jinns

5. **The Day of Judgement.**
   This takes place at the end of this worldly life, when all the dead will rise to stand for their final and fair trial. But only God knows the exact day.
   Good deeds will be weighed in the "balance" against bad deeds.
   People with good accounts will enter Paradise (Heaven) and those with bad records will be punished with eternal torment in the Fire (Hell).
   Judgement is one of the main themes of the Qur'an and is emphasised in about 14% of the verses.

6. **The Predestination of Good and Evil (***Qadr.***)**
   This is mainly a belief of the orthodox Sunni Muslims. It is the belief that all events whether good or evil are predetermined by Allah.
   Thus devout Muslims will always utter *Insha Allah* ("if God wills") when speaking of future events or plans.

Islamic Practices - The Five Pillars of Islam

1. **The Creed** (*Shahada*)
   Saying or confessing the creed in sincerity is taken as the proof that a person is Muslim.

   Kalimatu Shahada
   La ilaha ill Allah, Muhammad ur-Rasul Allah-
   (There is no god but Allah, and Muhammad is the Messenger of Allah)

2. **Prayer** (*Salat*)
   The performance of prayer five times each day and of other non-obligatory prayers.

3. **Alms-giving** (*Zakat*)
   Zakat is name of the "poor tax" or dues collected annually as required by Islamic law and in order to secure salvation. Each Muslim is expected to give 1/40 of his income.
   This money is used firstly to support the poor, but some also goes to the collectors and Qur'anic Teachers. It may also be used to help those in trouble because they have just become Muslims. Some is also used to spread Islam, to build mosques, start schools and clinics and even to fight "holy- wars".
   Muslims can also give whatever they choose to help the poor at any time and these alms are called **Sadaqat**. Alms-giving is believed to bring special rewards and to cleanse a person from sin.

4. **Fasting** (*Saum*)
   The fast lasts 30 days during the holy month of **Ramadan**, the lunar month during which the Qur'an

was revealed to Muhammad. The main purpose of the fast is to teach self-control against evil.

5. **Pilgrimage** (*Hajj*)
Every Muslim who is healthy and has enough money must go to Mecca at least once in a lifetime for the annual pilgrimage.

Muslim Prayer

Prayer is one of the most important duties of the Muslim. Only three times of prayer seem to be prescribed in the Qur'an, but it is recorded that in a dream, Muhammad was ordered to teach his followers to pray five times daily. The first prayer begins at sunset and is followed by the night, the dawn, the noon and the afternoon prayers. *Mosque* means "place of prostration" and is the place where the men gather to pray. The women are encouraged to pray at home.

Ablution

Before the Muslim prays he must perform his ablutions as specified in the Qur'an:

> Q. 5:7
> *"O ye who believe! When ye prepare for prayer, wash your faces and your hands and arms to the elbows; rub your heads with water and wash your feet to the ankles..."*

The assurance of forgiveness of sins through washing with water is further clarified in Islam. Abu Hurairah relates that the Holy Prophet said that when a Muslim makes ablutions and washes his face, the water carries away all sins committed by his eyes; when he washes his hands, the water carries away all sins committed by his hand; and when he washes his feet, the water carries away all sins towards which he had walked; and he emerges cleansed of all his sins. (Culled from Riyadh Salihin pg. 93)

If after performing the ablution, one even flatulates (passes wind) the ablution is violated and the ablution must be repeated otherwise Allah cannot listen to the Muslim's prayers.

Azaan-The Call to Prayer

After performing the ablution, the next thing to do before any obligatory daily prayer (*Farz*), is to call the other members of the Muslim community to prayer. The call is usually made with a loud and penetrating voice by the *muezzin* (the caller) who stands on a high platform, such as in a minaret of the mosque, for all to hear him. He cries out:

> *God is most great. I testify that there is no God but Allah.*
> *I testify that Muhammad is God's Apostle. Come to prayer,*
> *come to security. God is most great (Allahu Akbar)*

Each clause is repeated at least once and during the morning call, there is the reminder that *prayer is better than sleep.*

As a matter of fact, this act of calling with a loud voice, was not given by Allah to Muhammad in the Qur'an. This raises a number of questions:

Is it not surprising that Allah should fail to give such words to Muhammad after giving him the rites of ablution?

Is it a call to Allah or a call to the people to bring them together?

Who really advocated this call to prayer? Was it the prophet himself? Who composed the long hymn used in the *Azaan*? How many prophets did Allah speak to in Islam? Are there some more besides Muhammad-Ibn-Abdullah?

Adherents who subscribe to this mode of prayer, have sought to use the Bible as their authority since the practice is not mentioned in the Qur'an. Unfortunately for them, they cannot authenticate the *Azaan* in the New Testament for there is no evidence or any remote connection in the New Testament to support *Azaan*. It cannot in anyway be attributed to Jesus. (It is interesting to observe that people who do not fully believe in Jesus should try so hard to associate their practice with Him).

In desperation to find a credible Biblical connection, they point to the book of Nehemiah Chapter 9 verse 4. Reading from the first verse, we find the Jews expressing sorrow as they reflect upon their past, present and future lives and draw closer to Jehovah. This was the annual feast they celebrated called the Feast of Tabernacles.

It is during this celebration that we find among other things, the eight Levites calling **with loud voices to the Lord their God**. This is the only verse in the Old Testament that Muslim preachers can produce in support of the *Azaan.* For years they have been using it to persuade the unsuspecting public that the religion of Islam is in the Bible.

We might ask, did Muhammad simply copy from the Jewish religion? Then anybody at all could have done that and claimed prophethood. Are Muslims consistent- do they practice everything in Judaism? What exactly was Muhammad's relationship with the Jewish community? Did he not state that they were as much his enemies as the pagans? (Qur'an 5:85)

Do you think that the Levites who were calling out with loud voices to the Lord their God were facing the Ka'ba? If it is true that the Levites were doing the *Azaan* (addressed to their Lord), why did Muhammad feel free to change it and make Mecca the *Qibla* (the place to which one must direct one's prayers) instead of Jerusalem. How come that the prophet stopped facing Jerusalem in his prayers if he was so convinced that he must follow the Jewish practices for prayer in his new religion? Did he, in fact, know anything about Nehemiah 9:4. Did Allah even mention Nehemiah to him?

How then did Muhammad and his companions come up with the *Azaan*? If Allah never revealed anything about it to the Prophet in the Qur'an, then how come it is being practised? Does the Hadith have anything to say about the practice as surely this would be more convincing for the Muslim than a description from the Bible?

Hazrat Shah Waliullah has narrated that the Reverend Companions found it difficult to get people to congregate for prayer without some sort of proclamation or prior notice. Ways and means of achieving this purpose were therefore debated. Someone suggested the blowing of a horn but the Muhammad ruled it out for the reason that it was the practice of the Jews. Yet another proposal was made for the blowing of the conch (a large seashell) but the Prophet again disapproved of it, saying that it was the practice of the Christians. So on that occasion they had to disperse without taking a decision.

Later, Hazrat Abdallah Ibn Zaid received a vision revealing the pattern for calling believers to prayers. When he narrated it to Muhammad, the Prophet was pleased to confirm that the vision was genuine and hence the *Azaan* was put into practice.

Reference: Yaqeen International Journal (Pakistan) Vol 30, No. 22, page 260, March 22, 1982.

This again raises questions. If this debate did really take place and if Nehemiah 9:4 records that the *Azaan* was already being practised (over a thousand years earlier) why didn't someone draw Muhammad's attention to the fact? Why didn't they turn to the Old Testament to find an answer rather than dispersing without taking a decision. Isn't it also a contradiction that one practice (blowing the horn) was rejected on the grounds that it was Jewish while another (the *Azaan*) was adopted on the grounds that the Jewish Levites practised it?

If the Christians had not used the conch, would the Prophet have approved of it for his religion?

What prevented the Prophet from turning to the Old Testament for a solution to this problem, if indeed the *Azaan* really was there, rather than dispersing without taking any decision? Modern Muslims are saying the practice came from Nehemiah 9:4, whereas the Prophet who brought the religion, says that it came through Abdallah Ibn Zaid. Which are we to believe?

The first *muezzin* was Bilal, the son of an Abyssinian slave-girl. Muhammad is reported to have said, "The callers to prayer may expect paradise, and whoever serves in the office for seven years shall be saved from hell fire," (Mishkat book iv ch vi).

Postures In Prayer

Just as Allah forgot to give instructions to Muhammad concerning the call of his followers to prayers, so it seems that He also forgot to give him the postures and positions in prayers in the Qur'an. Nevertheless, the pattern set by Muhammad was followed.

The prayers consist of words of praise and requests for blessing. The Muslim begins his prayers by standing and facing Mecca. Inaudibly he says that he intends to recite so many *rak'as* or bowings. Then opening his hands, he touches his earlobes with his thumbs and says, "*Allahu Akbar*". He then proceeds to recite the prayers that go with the bowings. Lowering his hands and folding them with the right over the left, he recites the first chapter of the Qur'an (*Fatihah*) and a few other verses. Then he bows from the hips with his hand on his knees as he says, "(I extol) the perfection of my Lord the great." He returns to an upright position with "*Allahu Akbar*." After this, he gently goes down on his knees, and places his hands on the ground while he prostrates by placing his nose and forehead on the ground. In this way he shows his full respect and submission to Allah. He then sits back on his heels with his hands on his legs and his eyes down before performing a second prostration with the same words. This completes one *rak'a*. After the last *rak'a*, he pronounces the **Kalimatu Shahada**, then looking over his right shoulder, says, "peace be on you and the mercy of God" and then he repeats the same words looking over his left shoulder.

In the mosque, complete unity among the worshippers is maintained at each stage by following the Imam who leads from the front.

From such practices, it appears that the religion has been reduced in simple terms to postures and rituals. The Muslim follows these faithfully believing that he is fulfilling the greatest requirement of Allah and yet there is no evidence that Allah really sanctioned these rituals. Neither can the Bible give them any credence or support nor did the Christians from whom Muhammad drew some of his inspiration.

Over the years, Muslim preachers have always been emphasising that Jesus prayed with the forehead on the ground thereby trying vainly to connect him to the practice. So the ordinary Muslim assumes that this was the only posture Jesus ever used for his prayers. Others give the impression that Jesus actually came after Muhammad and therefore practised what Muhammad had already shown to the world. These are feeble attempts by Muslim preachers to deceive people. If we want to know the origin of these practices we can go back even before the birth of Muhammad, to the practice of the Arab idolaters. We would see that they also made *Sujuud* (ablution) as they worshipped their idols and not only that but they also converged annually at Mecca to make *tawaf* around the Ka'ba to worship the 356 of their gods who were kept there!

Muslims should search through the Bible very well before laying claim to certain facts in support of their religion. Jesus did pray with his face on the ground in Matthew 26:39. However, it would be extremely sad for someone to hold strictly to this and make it a rule for all their prayers, since it was recorded only once in the Bible. Jesus did not come to preach postures in prayers as the ticket to heaven.

If only they care to know, they would see that Jesus also prayed while kneeling without ever placing his head on the ground.

Luke. 22:41
"He withdrew about a stone's throw beyond them, knelt down and prayed."

He began the prayers and ended it on his knees, without putting his face to the ground. At another instance, he prayed standing and looking towards heaven.

John 11:41 (NIV)
So they took away the stone. Then Jesus looked up and said, "Father, I thank you that you have heard me."

As the Jews taught that God could best be worshipped only in Jerusalem on Mount Zion, so also Muslims believe that Mecca is the Holy City of Allah. The Ka'ba is the Holy Temple of Allah where He resides, and Safa and Marwa are the holy mountains on which Allah displays his bounties.

In his teaching, Jesus never made a rule regarding where to turn our faces to, nor about postures during prayers. In fact when the Samaritan woman questioned him on this issue, he gave the following answer:

John 4:23 (NIV)
"Yet a time is coming and has now come when the true worshippers will worship the Father in **spirit** and **truth**, for they are the kind of worshippers the Father seeks. God is Spirit, and his worshippers must worship Him in Spirit and in truth."

As far as Jesus was concerned, the important thing in worshipping God is not the posture adopted and therefore, he never prescribed nor practised any one particular posture. Jesus **never** practised the religion of Muhammad and yet he showed us how to be a true Muslim, by submitting his will fully to God and **not** through the performance of ablution and postures.

Even in Islam, when the Qur'an mentions a Muslim, does it refer to someone who wears a "Batakari" (long tunic or robe), with long beard, performing ablution and facing east while praying? What good is it for a person to keep the "correct postures" and place his head on the ground while at the same time hiding knives, talisman, lottery papers under his Batakari and fornication, adultery and hatred in his heart? Do you think that Allah views such a person as a Muslim?

Since Christians have been admonished to worship God in spirit and truth, Muslim preachers cannot use the Qur'an and the Hadith to persuade them to now add certain postures to make their worship acceptable and their prayers effective. Unfortunately, some poorly taught Christians have been led astray and taken up practices like the wearing of a Batakari, removal of shoes during prayers, ablution and the rest on the grounds that they are all found in the Bible. However, careful study shows that these practices were not performed in the same way as they are by Muslims. Nor did God intend for them to be continued. They were rather ceremonial practices that pointed to the spiritual distance between mankind and God. With the coming of Christ and his complete fulfilment of the Law, the barrier between mankind and God is removed and the believer is set free to worship God in spirit rather than through ceremonial rituals.

Christians have not made a mistake in their mode of worship. If they are not seen to be praying five times a day, it is because they are praying continually and can pray at any time and in any and every situation. Our prayers are answered because our God is a prayer-answering God who delights to come to the aid of His children. We do not look east to Mecca, nor to Jerusalem for that matter, but God shows his power to us. In fact, there is nothing lacking in Christianity that can be learnt from Islamic religion. The Prophet himself had to learn from the Christians and the Jews.

As we listen to Muslim preachers, we often wonder what would have been the condition of the religion brought by Muhammad, if the Bible had not been in existence? For in practice, Muslim preachers seem to rely more on the Bible than the Qur'an to substantiate almost all rituals and practices in Islam.

Use of Beads

Muslims are often seen carrying a set of 99 beads strung in a circle. These are used to help them to remember the 99 names of Allah. Many Muslims believe that if they repeat these names they will get special help from Allah. Some have even taught that by repeating an appropriate name a hundred times, a Muslim can gain something from the meaning of that name. For instance if one repeats *Ar-rahim* "the Merciful," a hundred times after morning prayer everyone will be friendly to him; or if he repeats *Al-Haqq* "the Truth," he will be able to find something that he has lost.

Hajj – The Pilgrimage To Mecca - Rituals Involved

1. **Ihram:**

   Ihram means, "prohibiting" and refers to both the state and the dress in which the pilgrim enters Mecca to begin the hajj. Having bathed his whole body, the pilgrim puts on two long, plain, white cloths. One is tied around his waist to cover his legs to just below the knees and the other is wrapped around the top half of his body leaving the head and left arm and shoulder uncovered. While in this state, the pilgrim is prohibited from:

   (a)   Foul talk
   (b)   Sexual intercourse
   (c)   Quarrels or disputes
   (d)   Cutting of nails and hair

2. **Tawaf:**
On arrival in Mecca, the first act the pilgrim does after performing ablution is to make seven circuits around the Ka'ba, known as *Tawaf*. He begins at the *Hajar Aswad* (The Black Stone), which he kisses or makes a sign of kissing. Then he makes three circuits in quick step and four at a normal pace, each time kissing the Black Stone as he passes it.
The *Tawaf* is made on three different occasions:

1. *Tawaf al qudum* - on the first day
2. *Tawaf al ziyarah* - day of sacrifice (obligatory).
3. *Tawaf al wadw* - time of departure

The Significance of the Black Stone
It is the cornerstone of the Ka'ba and stands as an emblem, representing that part of the progeny of Abraham which was rejected by the Israelites, but believed to have become the "cornerstone" of the Kingdom of Allah. From the Jewish view, Ishmael was looked upon as rejected, and the divine covenant was considered to have been made with the children of Isaac alone. While prophets appeared among the Israelites, no prophet appeared among the descendants of Ishmael.
However, it was from the progeny of Ishmael that the last prophet was to arise, as the headstone of the corner (Bu. 118:22). Therefore, the Black Stone was placed as the cornerstone of the Ka'ba' as a sign that the rejected Ishmaelites were the real inheritors of the Divine Kingdom. The Black Stone is believed to have been given to Abraham from heaven.
On day six, the pilgrim climbs to the top of Mount Safa, recites Sura 153 and confesses that there is no

other god but Allah and Allah is great. Then he runs to the top of Mount Marwa and repeats the same words before returning to Mount Safa and starting again. He climbs up and runs between the two mountains seven times. In the evening he returns to Mecca.

3. **Mounts Safa and Marwa:**
   On day six, the pilgrim runs between Mount Safa and Mount Marwa seven times. Every time climbing to the summit of each mountain and repeating Sura 153 and the creed.

4. **Mina:**
   On *Tarwiyah*, the 8th of Dhu'l-Hijjah, all the pilgrims move together to Mina, a plain that lies midway between Arafat and Mecca, about 4 miles from Mecca. The pilgrims stay here until the following morning and then after performing the morning prayer, they all proceed together to the plains of Arafat.

5. **The Arafat:**
   This is the plain that lies east of Mecca, where the pilgrims gather to listen to a sermon (*khutbah*) delivered by an Imam from a pulpit called *Jubal al-Rahman* (Mount of Mercy). If a pilgrim does not join the assembly at Arafat, his Hajj is considered incomplete.

6. **Muzdalifah:**
   The pilgrims then leave Arafat for Muzdalifah, which lies half way between Arafat and Mina. Its name comes from the word *Zalf*, meaning "nearness to Allah" (Q. 2:198). The pilgrims should arrive here in time for the sunset prayer and then spend the night before returning to Mina the following morning.

7. **Ramy Al-Jimar:**

   Ramy Al-Jimar means "the casting of stones" It takes place on arrival at Mina on the morning of the 10th day of Dhu'l-Hijjah. The pilgrims are required to throw seven stones at each of the three pillars called *Jamrah.* The first pillar is called *Shaitanu 'l-Kabir* -"the Great Devil." As he throws the stones, the pilgrim speaks out his hatred of the Devil, in the name of Allah. This action teaches him to hate evil and evil doers. It is also a reminder of the spiritual fight that must be waged against evil.

8. **The Sacrifice**

   The 10th day is known as the Day of Sacrifice (*Yawmal 'a- Nahr*). This is the day on which Eid, the "Feast of Sacrifice"-*'Idu 'L-Azha* is celebrated throughout Muslim world marking the day when Abraham was asked to sacrifice Ishmael, (not Isaac!).

   The pilgrim may sacrifice a cow, a camel, a sheep or a goat according to his means. He faces the animal towards the Black Stone at the Ka'ba, cuts its throat and calls out, "God is great! O God accept this sacrifice". He then returns to Mecca to perform the Tawaf again. This ends the period of Ihram and the pilgrims remove their white cloths and have their heads shaven.

   They stay to rest for some days during which they go and drink water from the sacred well of *zamzam* which they claim is Hagar's well. The Bible (Genesis 16:14) however, says that Hagar named the well Beer-Lahai Roi and that it was located between Kadesh and Bared.

   Many of these rituals including the Tawaf, throwing of stones and the sacrifice of animals were customs of pre-Islamic Arabs. However, the Muslims hold that these customs came down to the Arabs from Abraham and Ishmael who founded the Ka'ba. It stands to reason that Muhammad would have found it highly impossible to have completely rejected the beliefs and practices of his own people when he founded his new religion. He could not, therefore, do away with the Ka'ba and all its rituals that were so dear to the heart of the natives. Therefore, he retained those elements which were in keeping with the spirit of Islam.

Those who return from the Hajj keep the honorary title "the pilgrim" *Al-Haji.*

Islamic Law-*Shari'a*

Introduction and Meaning

In these days, we hear much about the implementation of *Shar'ia* law in countries or states where Muslims form the majority of the population. Indeed, we should be aware that a committed Muslim will never be content to live in any society until it is governed according to Shari'a. Nor is the Islamic missionary task (the process of Islamisation) ever finished until Muslims account for more than 50% of the population and Shari'a is in place.

Shari'a is an Arabic word which literally means "the way to a watering place" and is understood to mean "the Path to be followed." It is believed to be the path that leads to Allah and that Allah Himself showed through Muhammad, His Messenger. In Islam, only Allah has the right to ordain such a path and only *Shari'a* can liberate the Muslim from servitude to any other but Allah. It is for this reason and this alone that the Muslim is obliged to strive for the implementation of that path and no other.

Every Muslim is under obligation to live his life according to dictates of Islam as contained in the Shari'a. For every step he takes he must observe the basic distinction between what is right or permissible (*halal*) and what is wrong or prohibited (*haram*). In addition, a pious Muslim will want to know what actions are "praiseworthy" and which are "blameworthy," so that he can reform his own actions in order to please Allah. Thus, Islamic theology divides actions into five classes:

1. *Fard* or *Wajib:* a compulsory duty, the omission of which is punishable.
2. *Mandub* or *Mubah*: an action that is rewarded but the omission of which is not punishable.
3. *Jaiz* or *Mubah*: an action that is permitted but is legally indifferent.
4. *Makruh*: An action which is disliked and disapproved by Shari'a but which is not under any penalty.
5. *Haram*: An action which is forbidden and punishable by law.

The Sources of Shari'a

Although, Shari'a originated from the command of Allah, provision is given for it to be expanded or interpreted by mankind using analogical deductions and other processes. Allah is the Lawgiver and the whole Muslim community (*Ummah*, "nation of Islam") is His Trustee. The Ummah therefore has an authority to make rules but this is not an absolute authority to create laws. All Muslims belong to the "Abode of Islam" (*Dar al-Islam*) and form one vast homogenous commonwealth of people who have a common destiny and are guided by a common ideology in both spiritual and temporal matters. In this commonwealth, sovereignty belongs to Allah alone and every member must submit to Shari'a.

Every Muslim who is capable and qualified to give a sound opinion on matters of Shari'a is therefore, entitled to interpret the law of Allah when necessary. However, no Muslim leader or legislature can form an independent judgement when an explicit command of Allah or His Prophet exists. Not even all of the Muslims of the world together have any right to make even the least alteration to it.

The legislative function of deriving laws from the Book of Allah and the Sunna is vested in the "Council of Jurists" (**Ulama** and **Fuqaha**). They are chosen by and from among those who are experts in Shari'a on the grounds of their enlightenment and understanding of the needs of the people. Only they are able to make new laws when needed due to changing times and circumstances. The ruler(s) is responsible to the Council of Jurists and is alone invested with the executive function of ensuring the law is enacted through his appointed delegates.

The sources of Shari'a in order of their authority are as follows:

1. **The Holy Qur'an**
   Qur'anic scholars have identified about 500 verses in the Qur'an that contain legal injunctions. They deal with issues such as: marriage and its responsibilities; business codes; oaths and vows; punishments for crime; inheritance and wills; justice and human rights; principles of an ideal state; judicial administration, laws of war and peace. The Qur'an is regarded as the first authority and cannot be abrogated by other sources.

2. The Sunna

    Sunna (plural *Sunan*) literally means "a way," "practice," "custom" or "rule of life." It refers to the behaviour of Muhammad whose conduct is taken as being exemplary. The Sunna was compiled after the death of Muhammad from the reports of what he said and did. These were collected from his Companions (*Sahaba*) and formed the body of tradition that was first circulated orally before being put into writing in the Hadith. This is regarded as a primary source of Shari'a but it comes second in authority to the Qur'an. *Hadith* (plural *Ahadith*) literally means a "saying" which has arisen either from hearing or through witnessing an event. It is also used of the telling of something new. The Hadith, which is also known as the "hidden revelation" (*wahy khafi*) consists of the teaching of Muhammad. Firstly, this teaching was given verbally, especially in the case of his Companions who were made to learn thoroughly so that they in turn could teach others the message of Islam. Secondly, through writing to rulers and governors who were given instruction on specific matters, such as collection of taxes or forms of worship. Thirdly, through practical demonstration where what Muhammad did became the model for everyone else to follow.

    There are many collections of Ahadith in circulation. These arose because different criteria were used to test the authenticity of a saying. Of great importance was the character of the individuals who formed the chain (*Isnad*) through which the saying was transmitted from the Prophet. If a saying, when traced back, had only been reported by one of the Companions, it was regarded as dubious and therefore rejected. For various other reasons, many hundreds of thousands of sayings were rejected. For instance, Bukhari, whose collection is regarded as the most reliable, examined 600,000 traditions but only accepted 7,397 of them.

In general the compilers aimed to assemble those traditions which would give the clearest guidance concerning the beliefs and practice of Islam, so that the Muslim would know what things were permissible and approved and what were not permissible or approved. Out of all the collections made, there were six, which were made in the latter part of the third century of Islam, that gradually found favour with the later generations and were accepted as the six Canonical Collections (*Sahah Sittah*). These are:

1. The Sahih of al-Bukhari   (AD 870)
2. The Sahih of Muslim   (AD 875)
3. The Sunan of Ibn Majah   (AD 887)
4. The Sunan of Abu Da'ud   (AD 888)
5. The Jami of al-Tirmidhi   (AD 892)
6. The Sunan of al-Nasa   (AD 915)

3.   **The Ijma**

Ijma is defined as the consensus of opinion of the Companions of the Prophet (*Sahabah*) and the agreement reached on the decisions taken by the learned *Muftis* or the Jurists on various matters arising since the death of Muhammad. This is classed as a secondary source of Shari'a and must be founded on the texts of the Qur'an and the Sunna. As such, it has authority and cannot be abrogated by a subsequent consensus except in the case where it was based more on public interest and public welfare subsequently requires it to be repealed. It has an important role to play within Shari'a since it allows for progress and reconstruction.

The consensus is supposed to be based on the Qur'an, the instructions of Muhammad (*Qaul al-Rasul*), the actions and demonstrations of Muhammad (*Fi'l al-Rasul*) and the preaching and speeches of Muhammad (*Taqirat al-Rasul*). It is however, recognised that some of the actions of Muhammad were of a very special nature due to his calling as The Prophet and Messenger of Allah. Therefore, not all of his behaviour acts as a precedent for the ordinary person.

The means used to reach consensus are "healthy consultation" (*Shura*) and "Juristic Reason" (*Ijtihad*). Different categories of *Ijma* are recognised: *Ijma' al-Qawl* is the "verbal consensus of opinion", *Ijma'al-Fi'l* is the "practical consensus of opinion" on an action and *Ijma' al-Sukut* is the "silent consensus". If during verbal consensus, all the Jurists gave their assent by verbal approval it is regarded as *Ijma 'al-'Azimah*, "regular consensus of opinion". However, if the issue is raised but none of them says anything it is *Ijma'al-Rukhsah*, "irregular consensus of opinion." Again if during practical consensus, if one Jurist does something and none of the others challenge him it is regular consensus, but if one does something and one or more of the others challenge him, it is irregular consensus. All of these forms of consensus are valid as far as the Islamic Law is concerned. A juridicial opinion or decision on any matter is called a *Fatwa*.

There has been much debate as to who can sanction *Ijma*, how many Jurists are required to ratify it and who can repeal it.

4. **The Qiyas**

Qiyas is analogical deduction which is used to decide on matters not specifically found in the Qur'an or

Sunna. As such, it provides a way of dealing with issues that arise due to the developments that take place in society as history moves forward. Like the Ijma it is a secondary source and is supposed to be based on very strict, logical and systematic principles. It must be based on the Qur'an, the Sunna and the Ijma.

An example would be the decision of what punishment should be given to one caught drinking alcohol since this is not stipulated by the Qur'an or the Sunna. The Companion of the Prophet named Sayyidna Ali concluded that the person who drinks gets drunk and when he has got drunk he begins to rave and accuse people falsely. Since the Qur'an states that the punishment for one who accuses falsely is eighty strokes of the cane, Sayyidna concluded that the person who drinks must also be punished with eighty strokes of the cane.

Shari'a and Non-Muslims

Non-Muslims living in an Islamic state are referred to as *Ahl al-Dhimmah* or *Dhimmis* which means that they are under the "pledge" of Allah, his Messenger and the Muslim community so that they can live under the protection of Islam. According to Shari'a, they are to enjoy all their human rights without any discrimination and this includes complete religious, administrative and political freedom. These rights are guaranteed in return for their loyalty and the payment of a reasonable tax called *Jizyah* which is used for the administration and defence of the state. This principle is founded on the following words in the Qur'an:

Q.60:8-9
Allah forbids you not with regard to those who fight you not for (your) Faith nor drive you out of your homes, from

dealing kindly and justly with them: For Allah loveth those who are just. Allah only forbids you, with regard to those who fight you for (your) Faith, and drive you out of your homes, and support (others) in driving you out, from turning to them (for friendship and protection). It is such as turn to them (in these circumstances), that do wrong.

This is interpreted to mean that Muslims must deal kindly and justly with unbelievers unless they are out to destroy Muslims and their faith. In respect to the "People of the Book," (Jews and Christians), they are given a special position because their religions are based on the Taurat and Injil which are regarded as Heavenly Books. Thus Allah said:

Q.29:46
And dispute ye not with the People of the Book except with means better (than mere disputation), unless it be with those of them who inflict wrong (and injury): But say, "We believe in the Revelation which has come down to us and in that which came down to you; our Allah and your Allah is One; and it is to Him we bow (in Islam)."

However, all this depends on the willingness of the non-Muslims to submit themselves to the Muslim state:

Q. 9:29
Fight those who believe not in Allah nor the Last Day, nor hold that forbidden which hath been forbidden by Allah and His Apostle, nor acknowledge the Religion of Truth, (even if they are) of the People of the Book, until they pay the Jizya with willing submission, and feel themselves subdued.

One can see how Christians living in Muslim states can fall foul of these provisions as their attempts to share the gospel can be seen as an act of rebellion and a conspiracy to destroy the state and the Islamic faith. Christians therefore need to be very wise and avoid the use of military terms (such as "crusade," "target," "beachhead," "spying out the land" etc) when describing their activities in Muslim countries and communities.

Marriage with Non-Muslims

Sadly, many people including Christians are not aware of the implications of marrying a Muslim and not a few have entered into such unions lightly only to reap disastrous consequences.

Islamic law allows Muslim men to marry women of the "People of the Book, *Ahl-al-Kitab*, that is Christian and Jewish women, but a Muslim woman is not allowed to marry a non-Muslim man. The Ottoman law of family rights of 1917 continues to be applied in some parts of the Middle East. It declares that marriage between a Muslim woman and a non-Muslim man is void. However, it is silent about the marriage of a Muslim man to a non-Muslim whatever the religion. In this respect, it makes no distinction between "People of the Book," polytheists or unbelievers.

According to Shari'a, apostasy by one of the spouses brings an end to an Islamic marriage.

Islam allows limited polygamy of up to four wives but only if a man is able to treat all the wives equally. However, nowadays, polygamy is against the law and incurs penalties in several Islamic countries including Iran, Iraq and Pakistan.

Jihad

Jihad is derived from *al-Jahd* which means a "struggle" or "striving." It does not necessarily mean armed struggle leading to the shedding of blood, but it can also be used of the struggle against hardship or against one's carnal desires. There are other words in Arabic for war (*al-Harb* and *al-Qital*) and *Jihad* is only used in the sense of a "Holy War" in the Qur'an when it refers to unavoidable warfare made in defence against the imminent onslaught of enemies. Only warfare in these circumstances is morally justifiable. The Qur'an does not allow its use for the spread of Islam for this is to rather be by invitation and by verbal persuasion:

> Q.16:125
> *Invite (all) to the Way of thy Lord with wisdom and beautiful preaching; and argue with them in ways that are best and most gracious: For thy Lord knowest best, who have strayed from His Path, and who receive guidance.*

Permission for Jihad was given only after the **Hijrah** when Muhammad and his followers had to flee from Mecca because of persecution. Although they tried to settle peaceably in Medina, their enemies refused to leave them alone. It was thus during this time that the verses concerning Jihad were revealed to Muhammad. It was justified on three grounds:

1. Because innocent Muslims were persecuted for no other reason than that they said that Allah was one and for establishing a religious system which was quite different from the pagan system of Arabia.
2. If permission had not been given, the enemies would have destroyed the mosque of the Prophet, the place of worship in which the name of Allah alone was pronounced. The non-believers would have continued to force the believers to give up their belief in Allah and the Last Day.

3.   Permission was granted especially at that time so that the rule of Allah could firmly be established on earth. The enemies were trying to destroy the divine institutions of prayer and the poor-rate.

However, there is evidence to suggest that even in Mecca, Muhammad began planning how he would establish his rule and by what means he could enforce it and spread it influence. Rather than simply an escape, the Hijrah was in fact a deliberate stepping-stone towards the setting up of the religious order that Muhammad believed that he was called to establish.

Unlike the practice of the "five pillars of Islam," Jihad is not obligatory on every Muslim for all time. Even in the situation where the calls comes to do away with their enemies, those who respond will be seen as fulfilling the obligation of those who remain. However, in the following specific circumstances it does become obligatory:

1.   Once a man has gone for Jihad and is stationed on the battlefield, it is obligatory for him to continue fighting.
2.   If the enemies attack an enclave of Muslims, every resident will be obliged to come out and repel the enemies so that the Muslims are not wiped out and their towns are not ruined.
3.   When a ruler who is recognised as "just and pious" orders someone to join the forces of Jihad he must go without hesitation.

In these circumstances Jihad is obligatory on every Muslim male who has reached the age of puberty and who is sane and has sufficient means to maintain his family while he is away. Women too have their part to play in providing water for the warriors and nursing the wounded.

Some Sects Of Islam

Muhammad is reported to have prophesied that his followers would be divided into numerous religious sects.

Abdullah Ibn Umar relates that the Prophet said: "Verily it will happen to my people even as it did to the Children of Israel who were divided into seventy-two sects, and my people will be divided into seventy-three."

"Everyone of these sects will go to Hell except one sect." The Companions asked, "O Prophet, which is that?" He replied, "The religion which is professed by me and my Companions." (Mishkat, Book I, ch.VI: pg. 2).

The number has however far exceeded the Prophet's predictions, for the sects of Islam even exceed in number and variety those of the Christian religion.

The Shi'a

Literally means "Followers." They are the followers of Ali, the first cousin of Muhammad and the husband of his daughter Fatimah.

The Shi'as maintain that Ali was the first legitimate Imam, "Khalifah," or successor to the Prophet, and therefore reject Abu Bakr, Umar, and Usman, and brand the first three Khalifahs of the Sunni Muslims, as usurpers.

They are also called the Imamiyahs, because they believe the Muslim religion consists in the true knowledge of the Imam or rightful leaders of the faithful.

The Shi'as are also called Isna-ashariah or the "twelveans," as the followers of the twelve Imams, namely:

1. Ali — the son-in-law of the Prophet
2. Al-Hassan — the son of Ali
3. Al-Hussain — the second son of Ali

4. Ali Zainu' l-Abidin — the son of Al-Hussain.
5. Muhammad al-Baquir — the son of Zainu I-Abidin
6. Jafar as–Sadia — the son of Muhammad al-Baqir
7. Musa al-Kazim, — the son of Jafar
8. Ar-Raza — the son of Musa
9. Muhammad al-Taqi — the son of ar-Raza
10. Ali an-Naqui — the son of al-Tarqi
11. Al Hasan al-'Askari — the son of Ali an-Naqui
12. Muhammad — the son of al-Askari.
    He is otherwise known as the Imam Mahdi and is said to
    have disappeared sometime between 873 and 880. The
    Shi'as believe that he is still alive but has withdrawn for
    a time and they, therefore, refer to him as the "Hidden
    Imam." They say he will again appear in the last days
    as the Mahdi, or "Guided One" who will restore peace
    and justice in the world before the Day of Judgement
    as prophesied by the Prophet Muhammad

The Shi'a do not accept the six correct books of the
Sunnis but they acknowledge five collections of their own,
namely:

1. Al-Kafi
2. Manalayastalizirahu' l-Faqih
3. Tahzib
4. Istibsar
5. Nahiju' l-Balaghah

The Shi'a have a profound veneration of the Khalifah
Ali, and some of their sects regard him as an incarnation of
divinity, while they all assert that, next to the prophet, Ali
is the most perfect and excellent of men.

After the twelve Imams, the Shi'a look up to the
Mujtahids or "Enlightened Doctors" whose opinion is final

in matters of Muslim law and doctrine. These doctors are appointed in Persia and confirmed by the King.

The Sunni

Literally means "One of the path." The Sunni applies to the large sect of Muslims who acknowledge the first four Khalifahs, namely Abu Bakr, Oman, Usman and Ali, to have been the rightful successors of Muhammad. They accept the Sihahu's Sittah, or "six authentic" books of tradition, namely Sahih Bukhari, Sahih Muslim, Sunan Abu Daawud, Jamial Tirmidzi, Sunan Nisaai and Sunan Ibn Majah.

They belong to one of the four schools of jurisprudence founded by Imam Abu Hanifa, Imam ash-Shafi, Imam Malik, or Imam Ahmad Ibn Hanbal. In Arabic they are called Ahlu Sunnah, "The people of the Path."

Sunnis by far constitute the greatest proportion of the Muslim population the world over. They are about 85% of all Muslims.

Among the Sunnis, Abu Hanifah is regarded as the Father of the Sunni Code of Muslim law.

Sufism

This began as popular movement among the uneducated masses in reaction against the growth of the elaborate theology of orthodox Islam. They desired to know God so they followed the example of the Syrian Christian monks who wore simple clothes made of wool (*suf,*) hence the name *Sufi*. Like the monks, they practised mysticism and asceticism and they pursued personal revelation. They were pre-occupied with contemplation of the "Divine Perfection" and they addressed God as the "Eternal Beloved."

The Sufis sought release from the ritual bondage of Islamic law. They preferred to worship with joy, dancing and feasting and often entered ecstatic trances-eg the "whirling-dervishes."

They were disdained by Sunnis and Shi'as but by the 12th century there was a general drift of Islamic thought towards Sufism. It was also out of Sufism that the *Shaikh* arose as the teacher of disciples.

The Ahmadiyya Movement

This Islamic movement was founded in 1889 by Mirza Ghulam Ahmad al Qadiani who was born in Qadian in 1835 and who died in 1908. His father's name was Ghulam Murtaza, and his grandfather was Ata Muhammad.

According to Ghulam Ahmad, his father occupied a chair in the Council of the Government. He was one of those who was loyal to the English government so much so that he helped it against the Mutiny of 1857, (a well-known rising against imperialism in the Indian sub-continent).

His father belonged to the Shi'a sect, but Ghulam Ahmad decided to disregard this and establish a new sect. His followers however, find no fault in the action of their founder and yet, whoever renounces the Ahmadi faith is seen as a rebel. Ghulam Ahmad was well acquainted with Islam and other religions. Therefore, knowing that Christians, Jews and Muslims were looking forward to the coming of a Messiah or Imam, in 1889 he proclaimed himself to be the one they were all expecting. He said that he was the Imam Mahdi and that in his person Christ had returned to earth to destroy *Dajjal* (the anti-Christ) and to establish the Kingdom of God. He also identified himself with the Hindu god Krishna. According to him, *Jihad* was not war against unbelievers but a spiritual struggle to overcome evil. He maintained the Qur'an, the Hadith and the four Sunni Imams and justified *pardah* for women.

The Ahmadis believe that theirs is the only sect which is acceptable to Allah and His Prophet and therefore condemn all other Muslims and Christians. They teach that Jesus did not die on the cross, he simply went into a swoon (faint) and he did not ascend to heaven. They explain his disappearance by teaching that after his recovery, he travelled to India and continued to preach there until he was 120 years old. Then he died and was buried like the rest of the Prophets and his grave can be found in Kashmir. They believe in the Qur'an and teach that no verse can be abrogated arguing that any apparent inconsistency between verses is due to faulty exegesis. Belief in Ghulam Ahmad as the Messiah-Mahdi is an essential article of faith.

The headquarters of the movement remained in Pakistan till 1974, when the Muslim World League passed a law stating that they were not to be recognised as Muslims. The movement could not stand the persecutions that followed the enactment of this law, resulting in the transfer of their headquarters from Pakistan to London (Britain being their colonial allies during Ghulam Ahmad's time). Despite this opposition, they have become one of the most successful sects at propagating themselves by their missionary activity and have gained many thousands of converts throughout South-East Asia and in South, East and West Africa.

Wahhabism

Founded by the Mohammed Abdul Wahab (1761–1787). He belonged to the Hanbali school. He opposed the Shi'a and the Sunnis. His followers ransacked the sacred shrines of the Shi'as and captured Mecca and Medina. They founded the state of Nejad. Pilgrimage to Mecca was stopped. This movement was crushed by the Turkish Porter (Khalifah) in 1828.

Babism and Bahaism

In 1844, a Persian named Mirza Ali Mohammed proclaimed that he was *Bab* - the "gate," meaning that he was the Imam Mahdi. He preached against the ritualism of orthodox Islam and proclaimed liberty to all men and women alike. This doctrine however, alarmed the government of the day resulting in his imprisonment and execution in 1850 plus the death of more than 20,000 of his followers in the persecution that followed. One of the Bab's followers, Mirza Hoseyn Ali Nuri, kept the belief alive. In 1863, he proclaimed that he was the long-awaited prophet. He took the name *Baha'u'llah* ("glory of God") and became the founder of the Baha'i faith.

The central belief is that God is absolutely unknowable but has revealed himself through his appointed messengers, including Abraham, Buddha, Zoroaster, Jesus and Mohammad as well as Baha'u'llah. Thus, all religions are seen as equally valid. Love to God and to one's fellow is seen as the foundation of true religion. Bahaism is an eclectic religion that prescribes doing good to every one. War was banned, and all disputes were to be settled by negotiation. Ramadan was also abolished as was the wearing of pardah (veil) by women. The orthodox concept of Jihad (fierce struggle) was also given up and slave traffic was stopped.

Quiz

Questions on the Origin and Meaning of Islam

1. What does Islam mean?
2. When did Islam begin?
3. Who was the founder of Islam?
4. Where was Islam first introduced?
5. Who is Allah?
6. What was the religion of Arabia before Islam?
7. Who is a Muslim?
8. Are Christians Muslims? Explain your answer.
9. What makes a person a Muslim?
10. Which of the Prophets was sinless?
11. Why do people sin?

Questions on Muhammad

1. When was Muhammad born?
2. Who gave Muhammad his name and what does it mean?
3. Is Muhammad a prophetic name?
4. How many wives did Muhammad marry?
5. Who was his first wife?
6. Who was his favourite wife?
7. Why did he leave Mecca and go to Medina?
8. Was he the first messenger of God to Arabia?
9. Which messengers appeared in Arabia before him?
10. What was the religion of Muhammad before Islam?
11. What is the meaning of Abdullah?
12. Compare the farewell message of Muhammad to his people with what Jesus told his disciples.
13. What prompted Muhammad to reserve a space for the grave of Jesus?

14. Will Muhammad come back again?
15. "Muhammad is greater than all the Prophets." Discuss.
16. Is Muhammad the Prophet foretold in Deuteronomy 18:18? Discuss.

Questions on Islamic Beliefs and Practices

1. How does the Qur'an represent the Trinity?
2. Do Christians believe in three Gods? Explain.
3. Is it enough to say that God is one?
4. Did the Qur'an come to replace the Bible?
5. Does the Qur'an contain all the truth?
6. Did Allah say that the Bible was corrupted and incomplete?
7. What are *Jinns*?
8. Why do Muslims perform ablution?
9. What is the *Azaan* and what is its origin?
10. Who introduced the pilgrimage to Mecca?

Questions on Islamic Sects

1. List the names of Islamic sects which you know.
2. Who are referred to as Orthodox Muslims?
3. List the differences between the Ahmadis and Orthodox Muslims.
4. Who was Ghulam Ahmad?
5. Who was Baha'u'llah?
6. Was Krishna a prophet of God?

BIBLIOGRAPHY

ABDALATI Hammudah   *Islam in Focus*

A.E.A.M:TEXT-AFRICA   *Taking the Good News to Muslims* (Nairobi: Evangel Publishing House, 1987)

ALI Yusuf   *The Meaning of The Holy Qur'an, Translation and Commentary* (Maryland: Amana Corporation, 1935, 1989)

DOI Abdur Rahmon I.   *Shari'ah: The Islamic Law* (Ibadan,: Iksan Islamic Publishers, 1990)

GILCHRIST John   *An Analytical Study of the Cross and the Hijrah* (Sheffield: FFM Publications, 1992).

GUILLAUME Alfred   *Islam* (Hamondsworth:, Penguin Books Ltd, 1982)

HUGHES Thomas Patrick   *Dictionary of Islam* (New Delhi: Cosmo Publications, 1986)

KHAN Majid Ali   *The Pious Caliphs of Islam*

MADANNY M. Bassam   *The Bible and Islam*

MASOOD Steven   *Jesus and the Indian Messiah*

NASSER Waleed   *Muslims   –Untouchable   or Reachable?* (Kaduna: Baraka Press and Publishers Ltd, 1996)

SURTY Muhammad I.H.I.   *Islam an Overview*

UTHMAIMIN M.S.   *The Muslim's Belief*

ISHMAEL

SHALL BE BLESSED!

ISHMAEL
SHALL BE BLESSED!

by

Ahmad Agyei

ISHMAEL SHALL BE BLESSED

Copyright © 2002 Ahmad Agyei

This edition 2011

Published by:

Integrity Publishers Inc.
P.O. Box 789,
Wake Forest, NC 27588
U.S.A.
info@integritypublishers.org

ISBN 978-0-9828630-6-0

Scripture quotations marked (NIV) are taken from the HOLY BIBLE, NEW INTERNATIONAL VERSION® NIV® Copyright © 1973, 1978, 1984 by International Bible Society. Used by permission of Zondervan Publishing House. All rights reserved.

All other Bible quotations are taken from the King James Version of the Holy Bible, 21st Century Edition, 1995 or where indicated, Authorised (King James) Version, 1769.

Qur'anic quotations marked (M.Ali) are taken from *The Holy Qur'an: Arabic Text, Engli sh Translation and Commentary* by Maulana Muhammad Ali, (Lahore: Ahmadiyyah Anjuman Ishaat Islam, 7th Edition, 1991).

Qur'anic quotations marked (Pickthall) are taken from *The Meaning of the Glorious Quran: Text and Explanatory Translation* by Marmaduke Pickthall (Karachi: Taj Company: undated)

All other Qur'anic quotations are taken from the The Meaning of the Holy Qur'an: Translation and Commentary by Abdullah Yusuf Ali, (Maryland: Amana Corporation, 1935, 1989, 1993 editions).

Printed in the United States of America

CONTENTS

FOREWORD

Genesis 17:18-20 (NIV)
And Abraham said to God, "If only Ishmael might live under your blessing!" And God said "...as for Ishmael, I have heard you. I will surely bless him, and make him fruitful and will greatly increase his numbers. He will be the father of twelve rulers and I will make him into a great nation."

God promised Abraham that He would bless his son Ishmael. Through the history of the Bible, God kept His promise. Firstly, God blessed Ishmael physically; he became the father of twelve sons as God had promised and his descendants became prosperous and powerful peoples living throughout Arabia. Then, secondly, God blessed Ishmael's descendants spiritually; in Isaiah it was prophesied that they would come to God's Temple to worship Him. This was being partly fulfilled by the time of Jesus for we read that on the Day of Pentecost that came immediately after Jesus ascension, Arabs were present among those who had come to worship God with the Jews. It was on that very day, that many of them came to worship God in a fuller way. For they heard the message of salvation in Jesus Christ, believed and received the promised Holy Spirit.

Today, we know of many descendants of Ishmael who have come into the same blessing and so we know that God is continuing to fulfil His promise to Abraham. On the other hand, we are convinced that there are yet many more who will come; so it is with great confidence and joy that we say, **"Ishmael shall be blessed!"**

It is indeed, the sincere desire of the author to see the blessing of salvation through Jesus Christ come to the descendants of Ishmael. Through his own experience, he knows that it is God's desire to enlighten all who seek Him in sincerity. It is for this very reason that he has written a number of booklets in the past to challenge Muslims to think through their faith. His intention is not to win arguments or score points against them, but simply to point them to the same gift of salvation and eternal life that he himself has received.

Sadly, some have misunderstood him and others have deliberately tried to paint him in a bad light as an enemy of Muslims. This is far from the truth for, on the contrary, it is because of his deep love and concern for them that he devotes his life to their welfare.

He has no regrets at all that he turned from being a Muslim to being a Christian. He has been through many trials but in it all he has known indescribable joy and peace that he never experienced before. He finds great fulfilment and much blessing as he serves his Lord, Jesus Christ, day by day. Having found something so good, he longs to share it with others!

This book is a compilation of his previous writings which have been largely re-written to make the content clearer and the reasoning more understandable. It is hoped that this will be a helpful tool for Christians to use as they seek to enter into discussion with their Muslim friends.

The author is convinced that Ishmael shall be blessed and it is his sincere prayer that God will use this book for that very purpose.

The author acknowledges with sincere thanks the help of Afua Asantewaa who edited this manuscript.

1

IN WHOM CAN
TRUE ISLAM BE FOUND?

Introduction

The word "Islam" is derived from an Arabic root-word **SLM** which simply means "submission" to Allah. It describes a state of total submission to the will of Allah by an adherent or devotee. In its true meaning, the state of devotion is expected to be absolute in all the ramifications of the word, both in word and in deed. Under what circumstances can true submission to Allah be achieved? Is Islam an exclusive right of any particular religious group?

    We often hear Muslims or followers of the path that was laid by Muhammad referring to themselves exclusively as Muslims. All other religions are branded "Kaffirs" or teachings of infidels or unbelievers. In the eyes of those who claim to be Muslims, all unbelievers are doomed for hell for deviating from the path. Does the Qur'an affirm this position? Who is a true Muslim? This question is the central theme of this chapter, as the writer seeks to provide answers from both the Qur'an and the Bible.

Who is a Muslim?

It is strongly believed in Muslim circles that all the prophets of God were Muslims and many also believe that Islam even began at the time of Adam. They argue that Islam did not begin with Muhammad but was perfected during his time. Their popular quotation to support this assertion is:

Qur'an 5:4
...This day have I perfected your religion for you, and completed my favour upon you, and have chosen for you Islam as your religion...

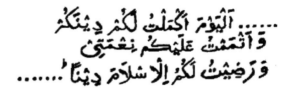

Supposing all the prophets were Muslims, (including Jesus Christ, who came before Muhammad), and also that Islam existed even at the time of Adam; then who was the founder of Islam? Can we claim that Muhammad was the originator? At best, he can only perhaps be described as the perfecter. For Muhammad to be either the perfecter or the model of perfected Islam, we would expect his Islam to be perfect (total submission) without falling short in any way at all. We will investigate whether this was so later.

Islam Misunderstood

Does a person consider himself a Muslim merely because of the set of rituals he follows, a particular kind of name he bears, or his mode of dress? No doubt the answer to this question is a big "No". We need to take note of the fact that Moses and all the earlier prophets never confessed Muhammad by reciting the **Kalimat Shahada,** ("There is no god but Allah and Muhammad is the messenger of Allah.") How then do we reconcile the claim that they were Muslims since recitation of the *Kalimat Shahada* is a prerequisite in Islam?

This raises a further question of considerable importance, which Islam did these prophets practise? Is it the Islam viewed in God's perspective as total submission or the Islam practised as a religion by the followers of Muhammad? Certainly, what God expected from the prophets, who are acknowledged as Muslims, was total submission to His Will. They were not Muslims because they were appointed as prophets, but rather because of their ability and willingness to submit to God.

Understanding Islam in this light makes us appreciate much better what God wants from us when we claim to be Muslims. This view is rightly in line with the Qur'anic injunction which states that:

Qur'an 3:85
"If anyone desires a religion other than Islam (submission to God), never will it be accepted of him, and in the hereafter he will be in the ranks of those who have lost (all spiritual good)."

وَمَنْ يَبْتَغِ غَيْرَ الْإِسْلَامِ دِينًا
فَلَنْ يُقْبَلَ مِنْهُ وَهُوَ فِي الْآخِرَةِ
مِنَ الْخَاسِرِينَ ٥

Does this statement mean that we are required to adopt Arabic names, assume certain postures and face specific directions in prayer before God accepts us as Muslims? If this is our opinion about Islam, then how do we reconcile this view with these words?

Qur'an 2:72

"Those who believe (in the Qur'an), and those who follow the Jewish (scriptures), and the Christians and the Sabians; any who believe in God and the Last day and work righteousness, shall have their reward with their Lord, and on them shall be no fear nor shall they grieve."

الَّذِينَ آمَنُوا وَالَّذِينَ هَادُوا وَالنَّصَارَى
وَالصَّابِئِينَ مَنْ آمَنَ بِاللَّهِ وَالْيَوْمِ الْآخِرِ
وَعَمِلَ صَالِحًا فَلَهُمْ أَجْرُهُمْ عِنْدَ رَبِّهِمْ
وَلَا خَوْفٌ عَلَيْهِمْ وَلَا هُمْ يَحْزَنُونَ ٥

The above statement clearly shows that being a Muslim means more than following prescribed cultural and religious practices. It shows that God does not prescribe Islam as an exclusive religion for, in that case, Christians would have to renounce their faith, change their names, recite the *Kalimat Shahada* and face a particular direction in prayer.

Some people think they achieve Islam by merely facing a particular direction in prayer and for that matter consider that as righteousness. What does the Qur'an say about this?

Qur'an 2:177
It is not righteousness that ye turn your faces towards East or West…

لَّيْسَ الْبِرَّ أَن تُوَلُّوا وُجُوهَكُمْ
قِبَلَ الْمَشْرِقِ وَ الْمَغْرِبِ ....

Qur'an 2:115
To God belong the East and the West, wheresoever ye turn, there is the presence of God. For God is all-pervading, all-knowing.

وَ لِلّهِ الْمَشْرِقُ و الْمَغْرِبُ
فَأَيْنَمَا تُوَلُّوا فَثَمَّ وَجْهُ اللّهِ
إِنَّ اللّهَ وَاسِعٌ عَلِيمٌ ٥

Some people also think they are Muslims because they wash certain parts of the body before praying to God and that righteousness comes through ceremonial cleanliness. Qur'an 5:7 is the usual quotation that is employed to substantiate the claim that this is the purity that God has enjoined:

Qur'an 5:7

"O ye who believe! When ye prepare for prayer, wash your faces and your hands and arms to the elbows; rub your heads with water and wash your feet to the ankles..."

يَٰأَيُّهَا ٱلَّذِينَ ءَامَنُوٓا۟ إِذَا قُمْتُمْ إِلَى ٱلصَّلَوٰةِ

فَٱغْسِلُوا۟ وُجُوهَكُمْ وَأَيْدِيَكُمْ إِلَى ٱلْمَرَافِقِ

وَٱمْسَحُوا۟ بِرُءُوسِكُمْ وَأَرْجُلَكُمْ إِلَى ٱلْكَعْبَيْنِ ......

The assurance of forgiveness of sins through washing with water is further clarified in Islam. Abu Hurairah relates that the Holy Prophet said that when a Muslim makes ablutions and washes his face, the water carries away all sins committed by his eyes; when he washes his hands, the water carries away all sins committed by his hand; and when he washes his feet, the water carries away all sins towards which he had walked; and he emerges cleansed of all his sins. (Culled from Riyadh Salihin pg. 93)

This is all that the Muslim understands he is doing when he washes himself before prayer. But, can sin be located on any part of the body? Can it be washed away with water? In which form does sin exist? What constitutes sin is found in the heart of man said Jesus the Messiah.

Matthew 15:18-20

"For out of the **Heart** come evil thoughts, murder, adultery, sexual immorality, theft, false testimony, slander. These are what make a man unclean."

Since the heart, although it is the seat of all evil deeds, is not included in the bodily parts that are washed, then the washing of the face, hands, nose, mouth, ears and feet is insufficient to make one a Muslim. After all, when one flatulates (passes wind), the ablution is violated and Allah cannot listen to you unless you wash yourself again. As if it is flatulence that separates us from God. Is it not sin that God detests in our lives as we claim to be Muslims? This is indeed what the Bible tells us:

Habakkuk 1:13
"Thou art of purer eyes than to behold evil, and canst not look on iniquity..."

Isaiah 59:1-2
Behold, the Lord's hand is not shortened, that it cannot save; neither his ear heavy, that it cannot hear; but your iniquities have separated between you and your God, and your sins have hid his face from you, that he will not hear.

Who then can be considered a Muslim before God?

Does your understanding of a Muslim refer to someone who has a beard, wears a long robe and touches the ground with his forehead as a sign of submission? It is ridiculous for some Muslims to say that Jesus was a Muslim for the mere fact that he had a beard, wore long robes, performed ablution and prayed with his forehead on the ground. If this is what makes one a Muslim, then what brand of Muslims should one expect? Did Jesus only pray in one way, always with his face on the ground? Did Jesus also wash his feet before washing that of his disciples? If only people would care to know, they will realise that Jesus also prayed while kneeling.

Luke 22:41
He withdrew about a stone's throw beyond them, knelt down and prayed

On other occasions, he prayed standing and looked towards heaven.

John 11:41 (NIV)
Then Jesus looked up and said, "Father, I thank you that you have heard me..."

John 17:1 (NIV)
After Jesus said this, he looked towards heaven and prayed...

As far as Jesus was concerned, worshipping God should be done in spirit and in truth. The mode and procedure is unimportant and cannot of itself make a person a Muslim. There is no proof that Jesus ever practised the rituals being advocated by Muslims. He never visited any holy city to run round stones and edifices in order to become a Muslim.

Daniel did not pray with his face on the ground; he prayed on his knees but his prayers were still answered by God. Our God should not be seen as a one-way God.

Daniel 6:10
Now when Daniel learned that the decree had been published, he went home to his upstairs room where the windows opened towards Jerusalem. Three times a day he got down on his knees and prayed, giving thanks to his God, just as he had done before.

Remember that Muhammad also initially prayed facing Jerusalem, not Mecca, when he was living in Medina. What led to his changing the direction from Jerusalem to Mecca?

The apostle Peter also prayed on his knees for Dorcas to be brought back to life again.

Acts 9:40

"Peter sent them all out of the room, then he got down on his knees and prayed. Turning towards the dead woman, he said, 'Tabitha, get up.' She opened her eyes, and seeing Peter, she sat up."

This verse clearly shows that the experience of God's power does not lie in one's posture at prayer but purely on the basis of faith in Him. Christians in Acts 21:5 prayed to their God on their knees, their faces were not on the ground and yet God listened to them.

Does biological birth make a person a Muslim? This is how scores of people come to identify themselves as Muslims without ever asking why they are Muslims.

In the light of all these observations we also need to examine the claim that all the Prophets were Muslims. If a Muslim is someone who has submitted or surrendered his will to God, we would expect that Abraham, Noah, Isaac, Jesus, and the other Prophets would exhibit this submission.

The Real Islam And How The Prophets Fared

Let us remind ourselves that submission to God (Allah), and only to God (Allah), constitutes Islam. Anything short of this is something else. One can call himself a Muslim only when one is able to submit his will completely to God and **not** to Satan. One has to listen to and follow the voice of God, and only God. The moment one deviates and listens to the voice of Satan, one becomes disqualified as a Muslim by God's standard even though the person may still be practising the rituals of ablution, prostration, etc.

The Prophet Adam

Islam by its definition began with Adam and so he was a Muslim. Adam continued to be a Muslim as long as he submitted to God. How did he fare? We need to examine his life. Adam remained in the Garden of Eden and as a Muslim listened only to the voice of God until Satan came his way. Then what happened? The Qur'an reveals a surprising truth that would help us see things clearly:

Qur'an 2:36
Then did Satan make them (Adam and Eve) slip from the Garden and get them out of the state (of felicity) in which they had been..."

فَأَزَلَّهُمَا الشَّيْطَانُ عَنْهَا فَأَخْرَجَهُمَا مِمَّا كَانَا فِيهِ ......

God spoke to Adam and his wife and gave them a command to follow:

Qur'an 7:19.
"Adam dwell thou and thy wife in the Garden and enjoy (its good things) as ye wish; but approach not this tree, or ye run into harm and transgression."

وَيَا آدَمُ اسْكُنْ أَنْتَ وَزَوْجُكَ الْجَنَّةَ فَكُلَا مِنْ حَيْثُ شِئْتُمَا وَلَا تَقْرَبَا هَذِهِ الشَّجَرَةَ فَتَكُونَا مِنَ الظَّالِمِينَ ۰

As a Muslim, Adam should have listened to God and not to anyone else. His will should have been **completely** submitted to God. **This is what we mean by Muslim, and this is what God expects from Muslims**. However, instead of submitting to God, Adam and his wife preferred to listen to the words of another voice:

Qur'an 7:20-21
Then began Satan to whisper suggestions to them…And he (Satan) swore to them both, that he was their sincere adviser.

فَوَسْوَسَ لَهُمَا الشَّيْطُنُ ......
وَقَاسَمَهُمَآ إِنِّي لَكُمَا لَمِنَ النَّصِحِينَ ة

Because Adam failed to listen only to God and instead turned and submitted to Satan, disaster came upon him and his wife:

Qur'an 7:22
So by deceit he (Satan) brought about their fall (Adam and his wife)…

فَدَلَّهُمَا بِغُرُورٍ ......

Are we going to argue that Adam was ignorant of the will of God before he fell with his wife? The answer is an emphatic "No!" The assertion that they were ignorant can never be true because God had given them a clear command to follow. God's judgement was:

Qur'an 20:121
"Thus did Adam disobey his Lord, and allow himself to be seduced."

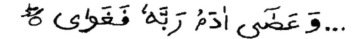

The words submission and disobedience are never synonymous, and therefore, disobedience to God cannot be seen as Islam nor can one who disobeys ever be worthy of the title "Muslim." Adam clearly disobeyed God. He refused to listen and submit to God alone, instead he listened to and submitted to Satan. In the light of his action, can we regard Adam as a Muslim in the real sense of the word? I know someone may say, "He turned back to God afterwards and God forgave him." However, the fact still remains that Adam did submit to Satan and thus, disqualified himself from being a Muslim before God. Hence his expulsion from the presence of God.

Qur'an 7:24
(Allah) said: "Get ye down...".

قَالَ اهْبِطُوا ......

We have realised that, although Adam was a Muslim, he could not submit himself perfectly and whole-heartedly to God. Satan was able to overcome him with his suggestions and ideas. Adam inevitably cried out to God as a sign of failure to measure up to the standard of God; and asked for forgiveness from God.

Qur'an 7:23
They said: "Our Lord! We have wronged our own souls: If
Thou forgive us not and bestow not upon us Thy Mercy, we
shall certainly be lost."

قَالَ فَبِمَآ أَغْوَيْتَنِى لَأَقْعُدَنَّ لَهُمْ صِرَاطَكَ ٱلْمُسْتَقِيمَ
ثُمَّ لَأَتِيَنَّهُم مِّنۢ بَيْنِ أَيْدِيهِمْ وَمِنْ خَلْفِهِمْ وَعَنْ
أَيْمَانِهِمْ وَعَن شَمَآئِلِهِمْ وَلَا تَجِدُ أَكْثَرَهُمْ شَٰكِرِينَ ٠

The "Muslim" in Adam became tainted and his Islam
fell short of complete submission and obedience to God.
Hence Satan was able to gain a victory in the life of Adam
according to his vow to take revenge against God.

Qur'an 7:16, 17
"Because thou has thrown me out of the way, Lo! I will lie in
wait for them on the straight Way. Then will I assault them
from before them and behind them, from their right and their
left, nor will thou find in most of them gratitude (for thy
mercies)."

قَالَ فَبِمَآ أَغْوَيْتَنِى لَأَقْعُدَنَّ لَهُمْ صِرَاطَكَ ٱلْمُسْتَقِيمَ
ثُمَّ لَأَتِيَنَّهُم مِّنۢ بَيْنِ أَيْدِيهِمْ وَمِنْ خَلْفِهِمْ وَعَنْ
أَيْمَانِهِمْ وَعَن شَمَآئِلِهِمْ وَلَا تَجِدُ أَكْثَرَهُمْ شَٰكِرِينَ ٠

The Prophet Moses

Let us examine Moses in the light of the claim that he was
a Muslim. How did he become a Muslim? Was he able to

submit perfectly to God without yielding to Satan in his life? Obviously not, for we see that Satan also played tricks on him and succeeded in getting him to act contrary to God's will. Moses at a point obeyed Satan and subsequently had to confess the fact with remorse and shock:

Qur'an 28:15
He said: "This is a work of Evil (Satan): For he is an enemy that manifestly misleads!"

قَالَ هٰذَا مِنْ عَمَلِ الشَّيْطٰنِ..
إِنَّهُ عَدُوٌّ مُّضِلٌّ مُّبِيْنٌ ٥

The fact is that, tragically, Moses was also floored by Satan and as a result, he also cried out for forgiveness:

Qur'an 28:16
He prayed: "O my Lord! I have indeed wronged my soul! Do Thou then forgive me!"

... قَالَ رَبِّ إِنِّى ظَلَمْتُ نَفْسِى فَاغْفِرْلِى

Moses is highly regarded as a prophet and as a Muslim. However, he could not submit to God fully throughout his life, without giving in to Satan. Satan was able to achieve his aim of causing all the descendants of Adam, as well as Adam himself, to sin against God. Moses therefore, joined in the ranks of Adam as one who had to ask for forgiveness for his sin. Yes, Moses sinned against God according to Satan's plot (Qur'an 7:16-17).

The Other Prophets

At this juncture, we need to remind ourselves that Islam means **total** submission. How do we then reconcile the occasional disobedience that became manifest in the lives of the prophets? In fact, God summoned a whole host of other prophets such as in Noah (Nuh), David the Prophet (Dawud) and Solomon (Sulaiman). Yet, God did not find one true Muslim among them who could practise Islam perfectly by submitting to God alone throughout his life. Contrary to God's desire, all these Prophets at one time or another in their lives also submitted to Satan and sinned against God. Each one, therefore, had to ask forgiveness from their Lord even as the Qur'an shows.

After sinning against God, this was how Noah also expressed his guilt:

Qur'an 11:47
"...And unless thou forgive me and have mercy on me, I should indeed be lost."

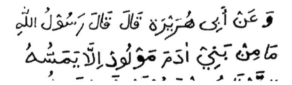

David also:

Qur'an 38:24
David asked for forgiveness of his Lord.

And Solomon:

Qur'an 38:35
"O my Lord! Forgive me.:"

$$\text{قَالَ رَبِّ اغْفِرْلِيْ} \ldots\ldots$$

How come that Satan was able to seduce all these prophets and cause them to submit to him, thus disqualifying them as Muslims? Can any of them boast that he was a Muslim? Satan would only remind them, "Have you forgotten how I caused you to sin by obeying my will?" It is worthwhile to note that, all the Prophets were "Descendants of Adam," ***Rusullum-min-kum*** (Qur'an 7:35).

Just as Adam was subdued by Satan, so also all his descendants came under the control and influence of Satan. We are therefore confronted with this inevitable question: **"Who among the prophets was able to surrender his will perfectly to God, and to completely subdue Satan?"** Do not think that we do not believe in or respect God's prophets. They were indeed God's prophets. However, that does not stop us from examining their lives to see whether they remained Muslims or whether Satan could ever accuse them of any sin. Did **any** of the prophets ever succeed in living without sin? Yes, there is someone among the prophets, who remained a Muslim without any sin whatsoever. Let us read what Abu Huraira reported Muhammad, Allah's Messenger, as saying:

> *"There is none among the sons of Adam who is born but not touched by the Satan at the time of his birth. So he cried loudly because of Satan's touch. But this is not the case with Mary and her son"*

وَ عَنْ أَبِى هُرَيْرَةَ قَالَ قَالَ رَسُوْلُ اللّٰهِ

مَا مِنْ بَنِيْ اٰدَمَ مَوْلُودٍ اِلَّا يَمَسُّهُ

الشَّيْطَانُ حِيْنَ يُوْلَدُ فَيَسْتَهِلُّ

صَارِخًا مِنْ مَسِّ الشَّيْطَانِ غَيْرَ

مَرْيَمَ وَاُبْنِهَا مُتَّفَقٌ عَلَيْهِ .

The above Hadith supports Allah's revelation in the Qur'an about Jesus' sinlessness even before his birth. For the angel announcing the birth said to Mary:

Qur'an 19:19
"Nay I am only a messenger from thy Lord (to announce) to thee the gift of a holy son.:."

قَالَ اِنَّمَا اَنَارَسُوْلُ رَبِّكِ

لِاَهَبَ لَكِ غُلٰمًا زَكِيًّا

Even before the birth of Jesus, the angels knew him to be holy, pure, sinless and faultless.

In the light of the above claim, Jesus stands out unique among all the prophets who were descendants of Adam. Hence all the others died and went back into dust according to divine law, *(Annaso kuluhum banuu Adam. Wa Adam min turaabin).*

The superiority of Jesus above all other prophets is underlined in the following verse.

Qur'an 4:171
"...Christ Jesus the son of Mary was (no more) than an apostle of God, and His word, which He bestowed on Mary, and a Spirit proceeding from Him..."

وَإِنَّمَاالْمَسِيحُ عِيسَى ابْنُ مَرْيَمَ رَسُولُ اللَّهِ ......
...... وَكَلِمَتُهُ أَلْقَهَا إِلَى مَرْيَمَ وَرُوحٌ مِّنْهُ ......

All the prophets, from Adam right down to Jesus, can equally be referred to as apostles or messengers of Allah. However, none of them takes the titles **Allah's Word** or **His Spirit** apart from Jesus alone. Jesus Christ never sinned because he is **Allah's Spirit** (*Ruhu'llah*). Since Allah's Spirit is holy, Jesus must also be holy even as confirmed by the Qur'an and by the ample evidence of his sinlessness in the Bible.

It was Jesus alone who overcame Satan. How did he do it? He triumphed over Satan by the cross. The devil defeated all the prophets, and there is no doubt about that. It was the devil who seduced all the prophets to disobey and sin against God – and thereby they were unable to surrender fully to God. Consequently, all the prophets asked for forgiveness of their Lord for the sins they committed. In contrast, neither the Qur'an nor the Bible ever records Jesus asking for forgiveness. That is because there was no sin in the life of Jesus that he should ever need to ask for forgiveness. On the other hand, it is recorded that Muhammad sometimes asked for forgiveness of Allah more than seventy times a day. This may sound unbelievable, but is quite evident

from "Riyadh Salihin" (pg.16) as Abu Hurairah relates that
he heard the Prophet say:

*"Allah is my witness, that I seek forgiveness of Allah and
turn to Him more than seventy times a day"* (Bukhari)

و عَنْ أَبِي هُرَيْرَةَ رَضِيَ اللهَ عنه قال:
سَمِعْتُ رسول اللهَ ﷺ يقول:
وَاللهِ إِنِّي لَأَسْتَغْفِرُ اللهَ وَأَتُوبُ إِلَيْهِ
فِي الْيَوْمِ أَكْثَرَ مِنْ سَبْعِينَ مَرَّةً ۚ رواه البخاري ·

The need of Muhammad to ask for forgiveness, as
reported in the above Hadith, is supported by the following
verses from the Qur'an:

Qur'an 4:105-106
*We have sent down to thee the Book in truth, that thou
might judge between men, as guided by God, so be not used
as an advocate by those who betray their trust. But seek
the forgiveness of God, for Allah is Oft-Forgiving, Most
Merciful."*

وَ اسْتَغْفِرِ اللهَ إِنَّ اللهَ كَانَ غَفُورًا رَحِيمًا ۚ

Qur'an 40:55 (Pickthall)
*Then have patience (O Muhammad). Lo! The promise of
Allah is true. And ask for forgiveness of thy sin...*

۰ ۰ ۰ ۰ ۰ ۰ وَاسْتَغْفِرْ لِذَنْبِكَ ۰ ۰ ۰ ۰ ۰

Qur'an 47:19 (Pickthall)
So know (O Muhammad) that there is no God save Allah,
and ask for forgiveness for thy sin…

وَاسْتَغْفِرْ لِذَنبِكَ ، ....

Qur'an 48:2 (Pickthall)
That Allah may forgive thee of thy sin that which is past and
that which is to come

لِّيَغْفِرَلَكَ اللّهُ مَاتَقَدَّمَ مِن ذَنبِكَ ....

This again confirms the fact that the prophets could not practise Islam (surrender their will to God perfectly) without any sin coming into their lives.

According to the Qur'an all the prophets were Muslims, but at a point in time in their lives, they chose to obey Satan and sin against God.

In an attempt to justify the title Muslim for the prophets, someone once remarked, "prophets of God do not sin, but they commit faults." Yet, the Qur'an itself has recorded that **they sinned** and therefore had to ask forgiveness from their Lord. What is the difference between sin and faults? When one sins against God, what prayer do we say? Who taught us this prayer of forgiveness? - "*Astagfirul-llaha Rabbi min kulizambin wa atubu ilayhi.*" What does the word "*zambin*" stand for? Did the Prophet not also recite this same prayer? How come that in his case and that of the other prophets, the word means "faults" but in our case, it means "sin"? Think about that!

The very fact that Jesus was the **only sinless one** among the prophets explains clearly why **he alone is the Messiah.**

Therefore it stands to reason that of all the prophets, he alone is destined to come back to the earth as a judge before the world comes to an end.

Read with me from the Qur'an:

Qur'an 43:61
"And he (Jesus) shall be a sign (for the coming of) the Hour (of Judgement)."

$$وَإِنَّهُ لَعِلْمٌ لِلسَّاعَةِ \ldots\ldots$$

If Moses, David, Solomon, Muhammad and the rest were to come as judges, Satan would remind them of their sins. They failed to practise Islam perfectly because at some point or other Satan was able to outwit them. Hence they failed to become Muslims in the real sense of the word. In complete contrast, Jesus actually practised Islam (total surrender) without any sin. This is the real Islam that God is looking for and in this sense, Jesus was the only true Muslim. Yet, you will agree with me that Jesus never confessed Muhammad in order to become a Muslim, nor did he journey to Mecca to strengthen his faith and fulfil the set requirements of the Islamic religion. No, Jesus was a Muslim because he never sinned against God and that is why he alone should be followed.

No Muslim will agree to be referred to as a Muhammadan because that word means "a follower of Muhammad." Muslims want it to be known that they worship Allah alone and that Muhammad only made the religion of Islam known. Yes, they are right. Likewise, one cannot follow Moses or David or any of the other prophets. The only one who can be followed is Jesus.

Sinlessness Of Jesus Christ In The Bible

Sinfulness simply means not being able to conform to the will of God; whereas the opposite, sinlessness, means complete conformity to the will of God. This is basically what Islam and Muslims are seeking to achieve. However, as soon as one deviates towards the path of sin, one can no longer be described as a Muslim or identified as someone who is practising Islam. Practising one's will and not the will of God can best be described as something else, it is not Islam.

It takes someone who has lived his whole life without committing even one sin to be able to claim that he is a Muslim and that he is practising Islam. Only Jesus can make such a claim for only he was able to live the whole of his life on earth without sin even until he was taken up into heaven (Q.4:158).

The sinlessness of Christ is best proved by the plain, inspired words of God:

> **1 Peter 2:21, 22**
> Christ…did not sin, neither was guile (deceit) found in his mouth.

> **1 John 3:5**
> And ye know that he was manifested to take away our sins; and in him is no sin.

We have encountered scores of people who by way of discrediting the scriptures, say they only believe in the "red-letter words"(the words spoken by Jesus) in the Bible. Thank God, John 8:48 is red-lettered: "Which of you convinceth me of sin?"

Christ was the only man with two legs, two hands, one nose and all the other human qualities that could ever make that claim honestly after Adam's fall. Jesus never admitted a fault or ever asked for forgiveness of sins.

"Did Jesus and his disciples not steal corn in Matthew 12:1-2?" This is the usual question posed by those who find it difficult to accept the sinlessness of Christ.

Did Jesus not curse the fig tree? Yes he did, but still he asks "Which of you convinceth me of sin"? Be careful, the question comes from Jesus so be mindful of your answer, for you stand to be judged by him in the last day.

The Qur'an clearly affirms the truth that it is proper to follow Jesus. He is the best coach to train you by his teachings and give you the power to become a Muslim. He alone is a Muslim in the real sense of the word and by God's standard.

Were you thinking it was not proper to follow Jesus? Come with me into the Qur'an.

Qur'an 3:55
...I will make those who follow thee (Jesus) Superior to those who reject faith, to the Day of Resurrection...

وَجَاعِلُ الَّذِينَ اتَّبَعُوكَ فَوْقَ ......
...... الَّذِينَ كَفَرُوٓا اِلٰى يَوْمِ الْقِيٰمَةِ

At this point, it has been proved beyond all doubt that Jesus was the only one who was able to practice proper submission to the will of God. Whosoever wants to practise proper Islam can do not better than to accept and become a follower of Jesus. If it is now your desire to follow Jesus Christ, to practise his kind of Islam (total submission to the will of God) and thereby, to become a true Muslim by God's standard, then I encourage you to invite Jesus into your life right now. If you do so, he will come and abide with you in power and your life will not remain the same again.

Please pray with me now:

Father in heaven, I thank you for sending your only Son Jesus Christ to come and demonstrate the true way of Islam to us. I now accept and willingly acknowledge that Jesus is the only one who lived a totally sinless life on earth and therefore he is the only one who has truly submitted himself fully to God. Your son Jesus is Holy because you are Holy. I do now invite Him into my life and humbly ask for His Holy Spirit to empower me so that I may also truly submit myself to God. Since He was able to remain truly submitted to God, I strongly believe that, with His anointing, I too will be able to do so. I know that this is His wish for my life.

Thank you for having come into my life to mould and transform me into one who is truly submitted to God as the Father so desires.

Thank you in Jesus' precious name, Amen!

2

THE QUR'AN IN
THE LIGHT OF THE BIBLE

Introduction

Muslim theologians have always emphasised the point that: the proof of the Qur'an is in its own beauty and nature, and the circumstances in which it was promulgated. As such, they have challenged the world to produce a book that compares with it but until this time no one has been able to do so.

Among the claims is the fact that the Qur'an is the **only** "**Revealed**" book whose text stands pure and uncorrupted today.

It is also a common saying of these theologians that: in the Qur'an, everything is explained in detail from various points of view, by commands and similitudes, examples, stories, parables etc. In other words, it does not merely narrate stories or lay down vague abstract propositions.

The popular view expressed by Muslim theologians is that the Bible, by all standards, has been corrupted and is therefore unreliable as the true Word of God. In its place, therefore, has come a **new** "revealed" Book that is authentic, and also enjoys extraordinary divine protection from corruption for all times. This belief is based on the **revealed** promise of Allah in these words:

Qur'an 15:9
We have without doubt, sent down the message, and we will assuredly guard it from corruption.

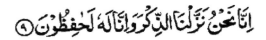

This divine promise needs to be examined carefully in the light of God's power and faithfulness. In the eyes of many people, the Bible seems to be more of human origin than divine. The content of the Bible has always been doubted by certain people who claim to know God. What makes the New Testament even more unpopular is the fact that some of the writers, such as Mark, Luke and Paul, were not among the Apostles originally chosen by Jesus.

It is the aim of this writer to now share some ideas on the Bible with you by examining its accounts in relation to those revealed in the Qur'an. It is hoped that in this way doubts shall be cleared and faith restored, in our effort to know the "Straight Way."

When Was The Bible Corrupted?

Allah has repeatedly emphasised throughout the pages of the Qur'an, that the book was "revealed" to confirm and fulfil the Bible.

However, when viewed critically, in many places and on essential fundamental beliefs of Christianity, the message given in the Qur'an aims at abrogating the message of the Bible. On the other hand, those who do not know much about the Qur'anic message sometimes assert wrongly that both books contain the same message. Even though some accounts appear in both books, the Qur'an is regarded as "**revealed**" and therefore unique in every way. There are others who believe that it was written by Allah Himself in heaven, and preserved, until Allah dropped it upon the Holy Prophet of Islam at the appointed time. Some also support the Qur'anic view that it was revealed in stages.

Realising that in many places the revelation in the Qur'an stands contrary to what is explicitly stated in the Bible, those who have put their trust in the Qur'an as their first authority have concluded that the content of the Bible has been tampered with. Consequently, they try to sift the content of the Bible and pick the flesh out from the bones. However, the problem is to identify the correct measuring rod for such an exercise. What should our reference point be?

Their claims imply that the Qur'an contains **all** the **truth** that was "revealed" by Allah in the earlier scriptures. But does the Qur'an provide **all** the truth that has ever been revealed? What message is Allah trying to convey to us by saying that:

Qur'an 4:164
Of some messengers We have already told thee (Muhammad) the story; of others We have not.

وَرُسُلًا قَدْ قَصَصْنَٰهُمْ عَلَيْكَ مِن قَبْلُ وَرُسُلًا لَّمْ نَقْصُصْهُمْ عَلَيْكَ وَكَلَّمَ ٱللَّهُ مُوسَىٰ تَكْلِيمًا ۝

This clearly explains why prophets like Isaiah, Joel, Micah, Jeremiah, Malachi, Haggai, Samuel, Hosea, Amos, Obadiah, Habakkuk and the rest; are not mentioned in Allah's message revealed to Muhammad.

Similarly, numerous events that took place as Allah began to reveal His purpose and will to mankind, also cannot be traced in the "Revealed" Book. This raises the question: How comprehensive and up-to-date can the message of the Qur'an be in the light of the above assertion?

Another important question to consider is this: if it is true that the Bible has been corrupted, did this take place **before or after** the revelation of the Qur'an?

Allah is all-knowing and wise. He does not make any mistake in whatever He says or does since He is fully aware of the past, present and the future. Therefore we are confident that Allah knew what He was saying in the course of revealing His message to Muhammad – as recorded in the Qur'an. Allah spoke these words in the Qur'an centuries after the "alleged" corruption had taken place in the Bible.

Qur'an 4:136
O ye who believe! Believe in Allah and His Apostle, and the Scripture which He hath sent to His Apostle and the Scripture which He sent to those before (him). Any who denieth Allah, His Angels, His Books, His Apostles, and the Day of Judgement, hath gone far, far astray.

يَٰٓأَيُّهَا ٱلَّذِينَ ءَامَنُوٓاْ ءَامِنُواْ بِٱللَّهِ وَرَسُولِهِ وَٱلْكِتَٰبِ
ٱلَّذِى نَزَّلَ عَلَىٰ رَسُولِهِ وَٱلْكِتَٰبِ ٱلَّذِىٓ أَنزَلَ مِن
قَبْلُ وَمَن يَكْفُرْ بِٱللَّهِ وَمَلَٰٓئِكَتِهِ وَكُتُبِهِ وَرُسُلِهِ وَ
ٱلْيَوْمِ ٱلْءَاخِرِ فَقَدْ ضَلَّ ضَلَٰلَۢا بَعِيدًا ۝

It is extremely clear that the scriptures that were sent to those before Muhammad must refer to those which the Jews and the Christians had in their possession at that time.

Having received the above message from Allah, did Muhammad then turn round to say in the Hadith that, the scriptures revealed before him were corrupted? Is Allah confirming an already corrupted message?

Furthermore, there can be no doubt that from the Qur'an, Allah regarded the Torah (the Jewish Law) which was in the hands of the Jews as authentic and reliable at the time Muhammad encountered them. For Allah questioned Muhammad thus:

Qur'an 5:46, 47.
But why do they come to the (Muhammad) for decision, when they have their own law before them?... There was in it guidance and Light...

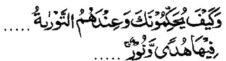

This shows that Allah Himself did not expect the Jews to seek light and guidance from Muhammad because He did not doubt that the Law that He had given them remained reliable and uncorrupted. The Holy Prophet of Islam never came to meet any of the earlier prophets alive, but Allah directed him in these words:

Qur'an 6:90.
Those were the (prophets) who received God's guidance. Copy the guidance they received

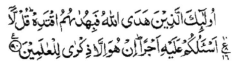

Apart from reading the scriptures received by the earlier prophets, there was no other means by which the Holy Prophet of Islam could have copied their guidance. Could Allah direct Muhammad to copy corruption?

It is also evident from the Qur'an that when the Prophet of Islam came into contact with Christians, their Gospel was still uncorrupted. In recognition of this fact, Allah admonished the Christians as follows:

Qur'an 5:50
Let the people of the Gospel judge by what Allah has revealed therein.

وَلْيَحْكُمْ أَهْلُ الْإِنجِيلِ بِمَا أَنزَلَ اللَّهُ فِيهِ وَمَن لَّمْ يَحْكُم بِمَا أَنزَلَ اللَّهُ فَأُوْلَٰئِكَ هُمُ الْفَٰسِقُونَ ۝

Which of the Gospels is being referred here? Is it the corrupted or the "original" one? It must be emphasised that the Greek text of the Gospel that Christians were reading during Muhammad's time is no different from the Greek text of the Gospel that is being read today.

So again we must ask the Muslim Scholars to explain exactly when the corruption of the Torah and the Gospel took place? Was it after the revelation of the Qur'an or before its revelation? If the corruption took place after the revelation of the Qur'an, then we would have to conclude that Allah broke his promise to safeguard His Scriptures. But as the Qur'an states, this is impossible:

Qur'an 3:194.
Our Lord! Grant us what Thou didst promise unto us through Thine Apostles, and save us from shame on the Day of Judgement: For Thou never breakest Thy promise.

رَبَّنَا وَاٰتِنَا مَا وَعَدتَّنَا عَلٰى رُسُلِكَ وَلَا تُخْزِنَا يَوْمَ
الْقِيٰمَةِ اِنَّكَ لَا تُخْلِفُ الْمِيْعَادَ ۝

Just as some Christians have slipped off from the truth of the Gospel, only to turn to the teachings of demons in our days, so it has been since the days of the Holy Prophet of Islam. Referring to this state of apostasy, Allah had this to say:

Qur'an 5:69.
If only they had stood fast by the Law, the Gospel, and all the revelation that was sent to them from their Lord, they would have enjoyed happiness from every side. There is from among them a party on the right course. But many of them follow a course that is evil.

وَلَوْ اَنَّهُمْ اَقَامُوا التَّوْرٰيةَ وَالْاِنْجِيْلَ وَمَا اُنْزِلَ
اِلَيْهِمْ مِنْ رَبِّهِمْ لَاَكَلُوْا مِنْ فَوْقِهِمْ وَمِنْ تَحْتِ
اَرْجُلِهِمْ مِنْهُمْ اُمَّةٌ مُقْتَصِدَةٌ وَكَثِيْرٌ مِّنْهُمْ سَآءَ
مَا يَعْمَلُوْنَ ۝

It is clear from these words that Allah wanted the Holy Prophet of Islam, as well as you and I, to be sure that the Law (Taurat) and the Gospel and indeed, all the revelation given to the "People of the Book" were reliable. Therefore He set it as the standard by which He expected them to live. What other Law could Allah be referring to apart from that contained in the Hebrew Scriptures and the Old Testament and what other Gospel than that of the New Testament?

What do you say about the Law, and the Gospel? This is what Allah commanded Muhammad to say about them:

Qur'an 5:71.
Say. "O people of the Book! You have no ground to stand upon unless you stand fast by the Law, the Gospel and all the revelation that has come to you from your Lord."

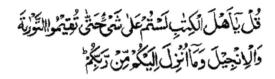

This again confirms the fact that the Bible is the standard that God expects Christians to live by. If God in any way doubted its reliability, why would He have made such a command? In fact, we can find no evidence at all that the Bible is corrupt and therefore we are confident that those who follow it are indeed the "party on the right course." We do not doubt that Allah is able to recognise such as these and to give them their reward even as He has promised.

Qur'an 2:62
Those who believe (in the Qur'an), and those who follow the Jewish (Scriptures), and the Christians and the Sabians, any who believe in God and the last Day, and work righteousness, shall have their reward with their Lord, on them shall be no fear, nor shall they grieve.

إِنَّ الَّذِينَ آمَنُوا وَالَّذِينَ هَادُوا وَالنَّصَارَى وَ
الصَّابِئِينَ مَنْ آمَنَ بِاللَّهِ وَالْيَوْمِ الْآخِرِ وَعَمِلَ
صَالِحًا فَلَهُمْ أَجْرُهُمْ عِنْدَ رَبِّهِمْ وَلَا خَوْفٌ عَلَيْهِمْ
وَلَا هُمْ يَحْزَنُونَ ۝

Allah was so convinced of the reliability of the Bible that He did not hesitate to counsel the Holy Prophet of Islam in this way:

Qur'an 10:94
If thou (Muhammad) art in doubt concerning that which we reveal unto thee, then question those who read the Book (that was) before thee. Vainly, the truth from thy Lord has come unto thee (Muhammad). So be in no wise of those in doubt.

فَإِن كُنتَ فِى شَكٍّ مِّمَّا أَنزَلْنَا إِلَيْكَ فَسْـَٔلِ الَّذِينَ يَقْرَءُونَ الْكِتَابَ مِن قَبْلِكَ لَقَدْ جَاءَكَ الْحَقُّ مِن رَّبِّكَ فَلَا تَكُونَنَّ مِنَ الْمُمْتَرِينَ ۝

The "Book" or the "Scripture" (Pickthall) referred to in the above Qur'anic verse came **before** Muhammad and must therefore refer to the Bible. This verse again confirms Allah's complete confidence in the Bible as a reliable source of His revelation. So much so, that He does not hesitate to recommend that Muhammad consult those who read it for confirmation of the revelation that Muhammad himself was receiving.

It is worth noting that Allah never instructed Muhammad to consult the Buddhists, Hindus, Confucianists, Taoists or the Zoroastrians. However, being sure of the authenticity of the Scripture of Jews and Christians, the beloved Prophet of Islam relied on them to the exclusion of all those mentioned above. Had it not been the uncorrupted counsel of Christians, the Prophet of Islam would have doubted Allah's revelation. Therefore, the uncorrupted Scriptures of the Jews and the Christians (the Bible), coupled with the reliable counsel of Christians, formed the sustaining basis for the Prophet in the course of receiving Allah's revelation.

The Prophet of Islam did not choose to consult Christians all by himself. The command came from the all-knowing Allah, who knew at the time of talking to Muhammad that the Scriptures of the Jews and the Christians were not corrupted. The Prophet therefore had no option but to obey Allah's command. In view of the teachings you have received so far about the Bible and the Christians, would you have encouraged the Prophet of Islam to consult Christians, if you were in this position?

Thus we conclude that Allah has set the Bible as the yardstick by which the truth of the Qur'an can be measured and ascertained.

Why then do men, who claim to follow and love the teachings of the Qur'an and the Prophet of Islam today, wish to go contrary to what the beloved Prophet did upon the instructions of his Creator? Surely, they do well to follow the recommendation that has come from Allah and take time to consult Christians concerning the meaning of the Bible and reliability of the Qur'anic revelation.

Perhaps you consider that Christians are lost and doomed for hell, but the fact still remains that had it not been for Christians, Muhammad would not have had confidence in Allah's revelation to enable him establish his religion.

Viewed against this background, I am sure Allah himself would not have passed judgement that the scriptures of the Jews and Christians were corrupted. Similarly, the angel Gabriel also would not have testified against the scriptures when he was sent to the Prophet.

Unless we all accept that the present Bible is still uncorrupted, we would be doing more harm to the

message brought by the Holy Prophet of Islam (P.B.U.H).
By attacking the present Bible, which is no different from
the manuscript that existed in Muhammad's day, Muslims
only do harm to themselves.

Therefore, since Allah has declared:

Qur'an 15:9
*We have without doubt, sent down the message; and we will
assuredly guard it (from corruption).*

$$ اِنَّا نَحْنُ نَزَّلْنَا الذِّكْرَ وَاِنَّا لَهُ لَحَافِظُونَ ۝ $$

then He, the all-knowing Allah wants us to understand,
this fact: **Just as He is able to keep the Qur'an from
corruption He has been able to safeguard His earlier
revelation in the Jewish Scriptures and the Christian
Bible from corruption.**

On the other hand, if we still maintain that the earlier
scriptures are corrupted and falsified, then indirectly we
are telling Allah that since He failed to guard the earlier
scriptures, there is no guarantee that He can guard the
Qur'an from corruption.

Is this not a reasonable assertion? The answer
obviously is a big NO, because Allah's power does not keep
on changing.

Who Corrupted The Bible?

According to Allah's own word, no one could have
corrupted the Scripture of the people Muhammad was
commanded to consult because Allah assured Muhammad
that:

Qur'an 18:27 (Pickthall)
And recite that which hath been revealed unto thee of the
Scripture of thy Lord. There is none who can change His
words, and thou wilt find no refuge beside Him,

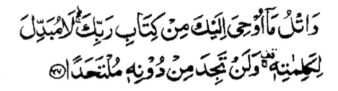

In the light of this, can anyone continue to argue that Allah could not preserve the earlier Scripture from corruption, the very same Scripture from which the Prophet of Islam received clarification? If they insist on maintaining this argument then we must raise the following questions:

If this same Allah, who could not preserve the earlier Scripture, should turn round and assure us that He can preserve the Qur'an, can we take Him seriously? Can Allah prevent men from introducing errors into His Qur'an this time? Won't He fail us even as He failed the earlier people?

If they are sure that He can protect the Qur'an, we want to ask, why could He not protect the earlier Scripture? Did He previously lose His power and authority or has He since lost His ability to protect His word? The answer is again a big NO.

During the time of the Holy Prophet of Islam, the Jews and the Christians were scattered all over the world, with their Scriptures. One may therefore ask, how was it possible for all the available manuscripts of Scripture to be corrupted simultaneously without leaving a single uncorrupted copy?

What do you think would have been the actual reason behind the alleged attempt by the Jews and the Christians to corrupt their Scriptures? Of course, this could not have been possible.

If ever there was the need for this corruption then, surely the Jews and Christians in Mecca and Medina would have done it, because they encountered Muhammad first. What about the millions of Jews scattered elsewhere? If the alleged corruption was effected separately, then it can be termed as nothing short of a miracle for all the corrupted manuscripts to have tallied.

Similarly, we cannot imagine the possibility of all the Jews and Christians gathering together for a consultative assembly to effect the alleged changes in their Scriptures because the Qur'an states:

Qur'an 2:113
The Jews say; the Christians have naught (to stand) upon; and the Christians say; the Jews have naught (to stand) upon. Yet they (profess to) study the (same) Book...But God will judge between them in their quarrel on the day of judgement.

وَقَالَتِ الْيَهُودُ لَيْسَتِ النَّصَارَى عَلَى شَيْءٍ وَقَالَتِ النَّصَارَى لَيْسَتِ الْيَهُودُ عَلَى شَيْءٍ وَهُمْ يَتْلُونَ الْكِتَابَ كَذَلِكَ قَالَ الَّذِينَ لَا يَعْلَمُونَ مِثْلَ قَوْلِهِمْ فَاللَّهُ يَحْكُمُ بَيْنَهُمْ يَوْمَ الْقِيَامَةِ فِيمَا كَانُوا فِيهِ يَخْتَلِفُونَ ﴿١١٣﴾

The enmity and petty quarrels that existed between the Jews and the Christians could not have allowed sufficient agreement for such a despicable act to be effected. In any case could they do such a thing without Allah's knowledge and against His own promise that He would preserve His words.

Dates of the Bible Manuscripts

Further to our debate, it would be very pertinent for us to consider the dates when the Biblical manuscripts were written. If we consider the Hebrew Scriptures (Old Testament) they were written over a period of over 1000 years beginning somewhere around 1450 BC. The first five books known as the "Law of Moses" or the "Pentateuch" were complete and regarded as canonical at an early stage and are referred in many of the other writings such as those of of David (1000 to 970 BC). The other two sections of the Hebrew Scriptures are the Prophets and the "Hagiographa" (the "other writings" -consisting of the historical, wisdom and poetical books). The last book written was Malachi around 435 BC.

The final compilation of the Hebrew Scriptures as used by the Jews is believed to have been done by Judas Maccabaeus in about 165 BC and a translation (known as the Septuagint) had already been made into the Greek language around 200 BC.

Jesus and the New Testament authors quote various parts of the Hebrew Scriptures as divinely authoritative over 295 times using both the Hebrew versions and the Septuagint (Greek version). That these Scriptures were the same as those contained in the Old Testament today was confirmed by the finding of the Dead Sea Scrolls in 1947. These 800 separate manuscripts, which belonged to the ancient Jews had remained hidden and well preserved by the dry atmosphere in the caves at Qumran from before the time of Jesus (probably from around 60 BC). They contain many portions of the Hebrew Scriptures and are the oldest original manuscripts available yet no significant difference has been found between them and the manuscripts which were used for the Bible translations made since the time of Muhammad.

If we come to the New Testament, we again find no evidence of the corruption that the Muslims are claiming. Through their research, in which they examine the writings of the early Christian Leaders and in which they note whether confirmed historical events are referred to or not, Biblical scholars are able to determine the most likely dates for the writing of the New Testament manuscripts. Here are some of the dates that have been determined for a range of the New Testament books.

Manuscript	Author	Place	Date
Gospel of Luke	Luke	Rome	about AD 59
Gospel of John	John	Ephesus	about AD 80
Book of Acts	Luke	Rome	about AD 60
Epistle to the Romans	Paul	Corinth	about AD 58
First Epistle to the Corinthians	Paul	Ephesus	about AD 55
Epistle to the Galatians	Paul	Antioch	about AD 49
Epistle to the Ephesians	Paul	Rome	about AD 61
Second Epistle to Timothy	Paul	Rome	about AD 67

From the above data, it can be inferred that almost all of the manuscripts of the New Testament had already been written even before the dispersion of the Jews in AD 70 and certainly before the end of the first century. None of the writers could have had any bias against the Holy Prophet of Islam since he was not born until some 500 years later. By the time he was born in AD 570, the New Testament manuscripts had been compiled and formed the sole authority for Christian teaching. A list of the accepted books of the New Testament (which is the same as that used today) is given in a pastoral letter by Athanasius which is dated AD 397. Not only that, but even before this time, the manuscripts had been widely circulated and translated into the Latin, Syriac and Coptic languages and quoted in the writings of the early Leaders of the Christian church. These writings confirm that the current New Testament is the same one that they were using. Thus it is not possible to maintain the argument that the Christians later forged the manuscripts to make *Periklytos* ("The Praised One" i.e. Ahmad or Muhammad), read as *Paraklētos* ("Comforter," John 14:16, 26; 15:26; 16:7) in order to destroy the Biblical support of the coming of the Prophet Muhammad.

At this juncture, let us examine some of the accounts that occur in the Bible we have today and compare them with what prevails in Qur'an as **revealed** to Muhammad.

Survey Of Biblical Accounts Recorded In The Qur'an

This section contains a survey of Biblical accounts which are also recorded in the Qur'an. The reader is invited to compare the accounts as recorded in the Qur'an with those of the Bible to see what conclusions may be drawn.

Old Testament Accounts

The Creation Of Mankind

Genesis 1:26
And God said, "Let us make man in our image,...."

Qur'an 2:30
Behold, thy Lord said to the angels: "I will create a vicegerent on earth."

وَاِذۡ قَالَ رَبُّكَ لِلۡمَلَٰٓئِكَةِ اِنِّى جَاعِلٌ فِى الۡاَرۡضِ

خَلِيۡفَةً .....

The Garden Of Eden And The Fall Of Mankind

Genesis 2:8
And the LORD God planted a garden eastward in
Eden; and there he put the man whom he had formed.

Qur'an 2:35
We said: "O Adam! Dwell thou and thy wife in the Garden;

..... وَقُلۡنَا يَٰٓـَٔادَمُ اسۡكُنۡ اَنۡتَ وَزَوۡجُكَ الۡجَنَّةَ

Genesis 2:16-17
And the LORD God commanded the man, saying, "Of
every tree of the garden thou mayest freely eat: But of
the tree of the knowledge of good and evil, thou shalt
not eat of it: for in the day that thou eatest thereof thou
shalt surely die."

Qur'an 2:35 (7:19)
*...And eat of the bountiful things therein as (where and
when) ye will; but approach not this tree, or ye run into
harm and transgression.*

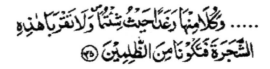

..... وَكُلَا مِنۡهَا رَغَدًا حَيۡثُ شِئۡتُمَا وَلَا تَقۡرَبَا هَٰذِهِ
الشَّجَرَةَ فَتَكُونَا مِنَ الظَّٰلِمِينَ ۝

Genesis 2:19-20
And out of the ground the LORD God formed every beast of the field, and every fowl of the air; and brought them unto Adam to see what he would call them: and whatsoever Adam called every living creature, that was the name thereof. And Adam gave names to all cattle, and to the fowl of the air, and to every beast of the field;

Qur'an 2:31, 33 (Pickthall)
And He taught Adam all the names...

He said:"O Adam! Inform them of their names, and when he had informed them of their names, He said: Did I not tell you that I know the secret of the heavens and the earth?...

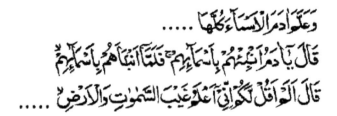

Genesis 3:1, 4-5
Now the serpent was more subtle than any beast of the field which the LORD God had made. And he said unto the woman, "Yea, hath God said, `Ye shall not eat of every tree of the garden'?"... And the serpent said unto the woman, "Ye shall not surely die; for God doth know that in the day ye eat thereof, then your eyes shall be opened, and ye shall be as gods, knowing good and evil."

Qur'an 7:20
Then began Satan to whisper suggestions to them, bringing openly before their minds all their shame that was hidden from them (before): He said: "Your Lord only forbade you this tree, lest ye should become angels or such beings as live forever."

فَوَسْوَسَ لَهُمَا الشَّيْطَانُ لِيُبْدِيَ لَهُمَا مَا وُرِيَ
عَنْهُمَا مِنْ سَوْءَاتِهِمَا وَقَالَ مَا نَهَاكُمَا رَبُّكُمَا عَنْ
هَٰذِهِ الشَّجَرَةِ إِلَّا أَن تَكُونَا مَلَكَيْنِ أَوْ تَكُونَا مِنَ
الْخَالِدِينَ ۝

Genesis 3:6-11
And when the woman saw that the tree was good for food, and that it was pleasant to the eyes, and a tree to be desired to make one wise, she took of the fruit thereof and ate, and gave also unto her husband with her; and he ate. And the eyes of them both were opened, and they knew that they were naked; and they sewed fig leaves together, and made themselves things to gird about. And they heard the voice of the LORD God, walking in the garden in the cool of the day. And Adam and his wife hid themselves from the presence of the LORD God amongst the trees of the garden. And the LORD God called unto Adam and said unto him, "Where art thou?" And he said, "I heard Thy voice in the garden, and I was afraid because I was naked; and I hid myself." And He said, "Who told thee that thou wast naked? Hast thou eaten of the tree whereof I commanded thee that thou shouldest not eat?"

Qur'an 7:22
So by deceit he brought about their fall: When they tasted
of the tree, their shame became manifest to them, and they
began to sew together the leaves of the Garden over their
bodies. And their Lord called unto them: "Did I not forbid
you that tree, and tell you that Satan was an avowed enemy
unto you.?"

فَدَلَّىٰهُمَا بِغُرُورٍ فَلَمَّا ذَاقَا الشَّجَرَةَ بَدَتْ لَهُمَا
سَوْآتُهُمَا وَطَفِقَا يَخْصِفَنِ عَلَيْهِمَا مِن وَرَقِ
الْجَنَّةِ وَنَادَىٰهُمَا رَبُّهُمَا أَلَمْ أَنْهَكُمَا عَن تِلْكُمَا
الشَّجَرَةِ وَأَقُل لَّكُمَا إِنَّ الشَّيْطَنَ لَكُمَا عَدُوٌّ
مُّبِينٌ ۝

Genesis 3:18,19,23
Thorns also and thistles shall it bring forth to thee;
and thou shalt eat the herb of the field; In the sweat of
thy face shalt thou eat bread, till thou return unto the
ground; for out of it wast thou taken: for dust thou art,
and unto dust shalt thou return... Therefore the LORD
God sent him forth from the garden of Eden, to till the
ground from whence he was taken.

Qur'an 7:24-25
(Allah) said: "Get ye down, with enmity between yourselves.
On earth will be your dwelling place and your means of
livelihood, —for a time." He said: "Therein shall ye live,
and therein shall ye die; but from it shall ye be taken out (at
last)."

قَالَ اهْبِطُوا بَعْضُكُمْ لِبَعْضٍ عَدُوٌّ وَلَكُمْ فِى
الْأَرْضِ مُسْتَقَرٌّ وَمَتَاعٌ إِلَى حِينٍ ۝
قَالَ فِيهَا تَحْيَوْنَ وَفِيهَا تَمُوتُونَ وَمِنْهَا
تُخْرَجُونَ ۝

Noah and the Ark

Genesis 6:13-14

And God said unto Noah, The end of all flesh is come before me; for the earth is filled with violence through them; and, behold, I will destroy them with the earth. Make thee an ark of gopher wood; rooms shalt thou make in the ark, and shalt pitch it within and without with pitch

Qur'an 11:36-37

It was revealed to Noah: "None of thy People will believe except those who have believed already! So grieve no longer over their (evil) deeds. "But construct an Ark under Our eyes and Our inspiration, and address Me no (further) on behalf of those who are in sin: for they are about to be overwhelmed (in the Flood)."

وَأُوحِىَ إِلَى نُوحٍ أَنَّهُ لَنْ يُؤْمِنَ مِنْ قَوْمِكَ إِلَّا مَنْ
قَدْ آمَنَ فَلَا تَبْتَئِسْ بِمَا كَانُوا يَفْعَلُونَ ۝
وَاصْنَعِ الْفُلْكَ بِأَعْيُنِنَا وَوَحْيِنَا وَلَا تُخَاطِبْنِى فِى
الَّذِينَ ظَلَمُوا إِنَّهُمْ مُغْرَقُونَ ۝

Genesis 7:1-2
And the LORD said unto Noah, Come thou and all thy house into the ark; for thee have I seen righteous before me in this generation. Of every clean beast thou shalt take to thee by sevens, the male and his female: and of beasts that are not clean by two, the male and his female.

Qur'an 11:40
We said: "Embark therein, of each kind two, male and female, and your family –

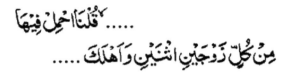

Genesis 7:10
And it came to pass after seven days, that the waters of the flood were upon the earth.

Qur'an 11:40
At length, behold! There came Our Command, and the fountains of the earth gushed forth!

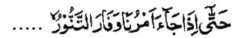

Genesis 7:17
And the flood was forty days upon the earth; and the waters increased, and bare up the ark, and it was lift up above the earth.

Qur'an 11:42
So the Ark floated with them on the waves (towering) like mountains...

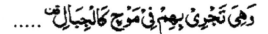

Genesis 8:1-2,4
And God remembered Noah, and every living thing, and all the cattle that was with him in the ark: and God made a wind to pass over the earth, and the waters subsided; The fountains also of the deep and the windows of heaven were stopped, and the rain from heaven was restrained;... And the ark rested in the seventh month, on the seventeenth day of the month, upon the mountains of Ararat

Qur'an 11:44
Then the word went forth: "O earth! Swallow up thy water, and O sky! Withhold (thy rain)!" And the water abated, and the matter was ended. The ark rested on Mount Judi...

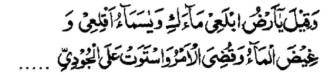

Genesis 8:15-16
And God spake unto Noah, saying, "Go forth from the ark, thou, and thy wife, and thy sons, and thy sons' wives with thee..."

Qur'an 11:48
The word came: "O Noah! Come down (from the Ark) with
Peace from Us...

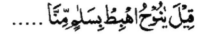

Abraham hosts angels

Genesis 18:1-7
And the LORD appeared unto him in the plains of
Mamre: and he sat in the tent door in the heat of the day;
And he lift up his eyes and looked, and, lo, three men
stood by him: and when he saw them, he ran to meet
them from the tent door, and bowed himself toward
the ground...And Abraham hastened into the tent unto
Sarah, and said, Make ready quickly three measures of
fine meal, knead it, and make cakes upon the hearth.
And Abraham ran unto the herd, and fetched a calf
tender and good, and gave it unto a young man; and
he hastened to dress it.

Qur'an 11:69
There came Our Messengers to Abraham with glad tidings.
They said, "Peace!" He answered, "Peace!" and hastened to
entertain them with a roasted calf.

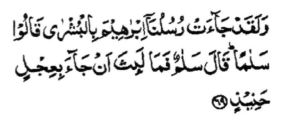

Genesis 18:9-12
And they said unto him, "Where is Sarah thy wife?"
And he said, "Behold, in the tent." And he said, "I will
certainly return unto thee according to the time of life;
and lo, Sarah thy wife shall have a son." And Sarah
heard it from the tent door, which was behind him.
Now Abraham and Sarah were old and well stricken
in age, and it ceased to be with Sarah after the manner
of women. Therefore Sarah laughed within herself,
saying, "After I have waxed old shall I have pleasure,
my lord being old also?"

Qur'an 11:71-72
And his wife was standing (there), and she laughed: but We
gave her glad tidings of Isaac, and after him, of Jacob. She
said: "Alas for me! Shall I bear a child, seeing I am an old
woman, and my husband here is an old man? That would
indeed be a wonderful thing!"

وَٱمْرَأَتُهُۥ قَآئِمَةٌ فَضَحِكَتْ فَبَشَّرْنَٰهَا بِإِسْحَٰقَ وَ

مِن وَرَآءِ إِسْحَٰقَ يَعْقُوبَ ۝

قَالَتْ يَٰوَيْلَتَىٰٓ ءَأَلِدُ وَأَنَا۠ عَجُوزٌ وَهَٰذَا بَعْلِى

شَيْخًا ۚ إِنَّ هَٰذَا لَشَىْءٌ عَجِيبٌ ۝

The Destruction of Lot's City

Genesis 18:23-24
And Abraham drew near, and said, "Wilt Thou also
destroy the righteous with the wicked? Perhaps there

be fifty righteous within the city: wilt Thou also destroy and not spare the place for the fifty righteous that are therein?..."

Qur'an 11:74
...he began to plead with Us for Lot's people

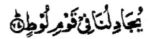

Genesis 19:4-8
But before they lay down, the men of the city, even the men of Sodom — both young and old, all the people from every quarter — compassed the house around. And they called unto Lot and said unto him, "Where are the men who came in to thee this night? Bring them out unto us, that we may know them." And Lot went out at the door unto them, and shut the door after him and said, "I pray you, brethren, do not so wickedly. Behold now, I have two daughters who have not known a man. Let me, I pray you, bring them out unto you, and do ye to them as is good in your eyes. Only unto these men do nothing, for therefore came they under the shadow of my roof."

Qur'an 11:77-78
When Our Messengers came to Lot, he was grieved on their account and felt himself powerless (to protect) them. He said: "This is a distressful day." And his people came rushing towards him, and they had been long in the habit of practising abominations. He said: "O my people! Here are my daughters: they are purer for you (if ye marry)! Now fear Allah, and cover me not with shame about my guests! Is there not among you a single right-minded man?"

وَلَمَّا جَآءَتْ رُسُلُنَا لُوطًا سِیءَ بِهِمْ وَضَاقَ بِهِم
ذَرْعًا وَقَالَ هَـٰذَا یَوْمٌ عَصِیبٌ ۝

وَجَآءَهُ قَوْمُهُ یُهْرَعُونَ إِلَیْهِ وَمِن قَبْلُ كَانُوا۟
یَعْمَلُونَ السَّیِّئَاتِ قَالَ یَـٰقَوْمِ هَـٰٓؤُلَآءِ بَنَاتِى هُنَّ
أَطْهَرُ لَكُمْ فَاتَّقُوا۟ اللَّهَ وَلَا تُخْزُونِ فِى ضَیْفِىٓ أَلَیْسَ
مِنكُمْ رَجُلٌ رَّشِیدٌ ۝

Genesis 19:12-13, 17,24-26

And the men said unto Lot, "Hast thou here any besides? Son-in-law, and thy sons, and thy daughters, and whatsoever thou hast in the city, bring them out of this place: For we will destroy this place, because the cry of them has waxed great before the face of the LORD; and the LORD hath sent us to destroy it."... And it came to pass, when they had brought them forth outside, that he said, "Escape for thy life; look not behind thee, neither stay thou in all the plain. Escape to the mountain, lest thou be consumed!"... Then the LORD rained upon Sodom and upon Gomorrah brimstone and fire from the LORD out of heaven; and he overthrew those cities, and all the plain, and all the inhabitants of the cities, and that which grew upon the ground. But his wife looked back from behind him, and she became a pillar of salt.

Qur'an 11:81

(The Messengers) said: "O Lot! We are Messengers from thy Lord by no means shall they reach thee! Now travel with

thy family while yet a part of the night remains, and let not any of you look back: but thy wife (will remain) behind: to her will happen what happens to the people. Morning is their time appointed: is not the morning nigh?"

Qur'an 15:56
"Then travel by night with thy household, when a portion of the night (yet remains), and do thou bring up the rear: Let no one amongst you look back, but pass on whither ye are ordered."

قَالُوا يَا لُوطُ إِنَّا رُسُلُ رَبِّكَ لَن يَصِلُوٓا إِلَيْكَ فَأَسْرِ بِأَهْلِكَ بِقِطْعٍ مِّنَ ٱلَّيْلِ وَلَا يَلْتَفِتْ مِنكُمْ أَحَدٌ إِلَّا ٱمْرَأَتَكَ إِنَّهُۥ مُصِيبُهَا مَآ أَصَابَهُمْ إِنَّ مَوْعِدَهُمُ ٱلصُّبْحُ أَلَيْسَ ٱلصُّبْحُ بِقَرِيبٍ ۝

فَأَسْرِ بِأَهْلِكَ بِقِطْعٍ مِّنَ ٱلَّيْلِ وَٱتَّبِعْ أَدْبَارَهُمْ وَلَا يَلْتَفِتْ مِنكُمْ أَحَدٌ وَٱمْضُوا حَيْثُ تُؤْمَرُونَ ۝

The Life of Joseph

Joseph's Dream

Genesis 37:9
"Behold, I have dreamed a dream more; and, behold, the sun and the moon and the eleven stars made obeisance to me."

Qur'an 12:4
Behold, Joseph said to his father: "O my father! I did see eleven stars and the sun and the moon: I saw them prostrate themselves to me!"

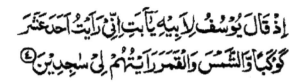

Joseph Interprets Dreams

Genesis 40:9,11
And the chief butler told his dream to Joseph, and said to him, "In my dream, behold, a vine was before me;... and I took the grapes, and pressed them into Pharaoh's cup,..."

Qur'an 12:36
"...I see myself (in a dream) pressing wine."

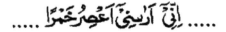

Genesis 40:16-17
When the chief baker saw that the interpretation was good, he said unto Joseph, "I also was in my dream, and, behold, I had three white baskets on my head: And in the uppermost basket there was of all manner of baked meats for Pharaoh; and the birds did eat them out of the basket upon my head."

Qur'an 12:36
Said the other: "I see myself (in a dream) carrying bread on my head, and birds are eating thereof

وَقَالَ الْأُخَرَانِّ ارِّسِّيَ أَحِلُ.....
.....فَوْقَ رَأْسِيَ خُبْزًا تَأْكُلُ الطَّيْرُمِنْهُ

Genesis 40:14,23
But think on me when it shall be well with thee,
and shew kindness, I pray thee, unto me, and make
mention of me unto Pharaoh, and bring me out of this
house. Yet did not the chief butler remember Joseph,
but forgot him.

Qur'an 12:42
And of the two, to that one whom he considered about to be
saved, he said: "Mention me to thy lord." But Satan made
him forget to mention him to his lord: And (Joseph) lingered
in prison a few (more) years.

وَقَالَ لِلَّذِى ظَنَّ أَنَّهُ نَاجٍ مِّنْهُمَا اذْكُرْنِى عِندَ
رَبِّكَ فَأَنسَاهُ الشَّيْطَنُ ذِكْرَ رَبِّهِ فَلَبِثَ فِى السِّجْنِ
بِضْعَ سِنِينَ ۝

Genesis 41:1-7 (1769 A.V.)
...Pharaoh dreamed: and, behold, he stood by the river.
And, behold, there came up out of the river seven well
favoured kine and fat fleshed; and they fed in a meadow.
And, behold, seven other kine came up after them out
of the river, ill favoured and lean fleshed; and stood
by the other kine upon the brink of the river. And the
ill favoured and lean fleshed kine did eat up the seven
well favoured and fat kine. So Pharaoh awoke. And he
slept and dreamed the second time: and, behold, seven

ears of corn came up upon one stalk, rank and good.
And, behold, seven thin ears and blasted with the east
wind sprung up after them. And the seven thin ears
devoured the seven rank and full ears. And Pharaoh
awoke, and, behold, it was a dream.

Qur'an 12: 43
The king (of Egypt) said: "I do see (in a vision) seven fat
kine, whom seven lean ones devour, — and seven green ears
of corn, and seven (others) withered.

وَقَالَ ٱلۡمَلِكُ إِنِّيٓ أَرَىٰ سَبۡعَ بَقَرَٰتٍ سِمَانٍ يَأۡكُلُهُنَّ
سَبۡعٌ عِجَافٌ وَسَبۡعَ سُنۢبُلَٰتٍ خُضۡرٍ وَأُخَرَ يَابِسَٰتٍ يَٰٓأَيُّهَا
ٱلۡمَلَأُ أَفۡتُونِي فِي رُءۡيَٰيَ إِن كُنتُمۡ لِلرُّءۡيَا تَعۡبُرُونَ ۝

Genesis 41:29,30
"...Behold, there come seven years of great plenty
throughout all the land of Egypt: And there shall arise
after them seven years of famine; and all the plenty
shall be forgotten in the land of Egypt; and the famine
shall consume the land;..."

Qur'an 12:47,49
(Joseph) said: "For seven years shall ye diligently sow as is
your wont: And the harvests that ye reap, ye shall leave them
in the ear, except a little, of which ye shall eat. "Then will
come after that (period) seven dreadful (years), which will
devour what ye shall have laid by in advance for them, (all)
except a little which ye shall have (specially) guarded. "Then
will come after that (period) a year in which the people will
have abundant water, and in which they will press (wine
and oil).

قَالَ تَزْرَعُونَ سَبْعَ سِنِينَ دَأَبًا فَمَا حَصَدتُّمْ فَذَرُوهُ
فِى سُنبُلِهِ إِلَّا قَلِيلًا مِّمَّا تَأْكُلُونَ ۝
ثُمَّ يَأْتِى مِنۢ بَعْدِ ذَٰلِكَ عَامٌ فِيهِ يُغَاثُ النَّاسُ وَ
فِيهِ يَعْصِرُونَ ۝

Genesis 41:40-41

"...Thou shalt be over my house, and according unto thy word shall all my people be ruled..." And Pharaoh said unto Joseph, "See, I have set thee over all the land of Egypt."

Qur'an 12:54

So the king said: "Bring him unto me; I will take him specially to serve about my own person." Therefore when he had spoken to him. he said: "Be assured this day, thou art, before our own Presence, with rank firmly established, and fidelity fully proved!"

وَقَالَ الْمَلِكُ ائْتُونِى بِهِ أَسْتَخْلِصْهُ لِنَفْسِى فَلَمَّا
كَلَّمَهُ قَالَ إِنَّكَ الْيَوْمَ لَدَيْنَا مَكِينٌ أَمِينٌ ۝

Joseph Reunited With His Brothers

Genesis 42:7-8

And Joseph saw his brethren, and he knew them... but they knew not him.

Qur'an 12:58
Then came Joseph's brethren: They entered his presence, and
he knew them, but they knew him not.

وَجَآءَ إِخْوَةُ يُوسُفَ فَدَخَلُوا عَلَيْهِ فَعَرَفَهُمْ وَهُمْ
لَهُ مُنكِرُونَ ۝

Genesis 42:25
Then Joseph commanded to fill their sacks with corn,
and to restore every man's money into his sack...

Qur'an 12:62
And (Joseph) told his servants to put their stock-in-trade
(with which they had bartered) into their saddlebags...

..... فَلَمَّا رَجَعُوا إِلَى أَبِيهِمْ قَالُوا يَا أَبَانَا مُنِعَ مِنَّا الْكَيْلُ

Genesis 42:35
And it came to pass as they emptied their sacks, that,
behold, every man's bundle of money was in his sack.

Qur'an 12:65
Then when they opened their baggage, they found their
stock-in-trade had been returned to them...

وَلَمَّا فَتَحُوا مَتَاعَهُمْ وَجَدُوا بِضَاعَتَهُمْ رُدَّتْ
إِلَيْهِمْ .....

Genesis 44:2
And put my cup, the silver cup, in the sack's mouth of
the youngest, and his corn money.

Qur'an 12:70
... he put the drinking cup into his brother's saddlebag

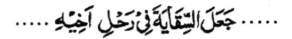

Genesis 44:4-5
...Joseph said unto his steward, "Up, follow after the men; and when thou dost overtake them, say unto them, `Why have ye rewarded evil for good? Is not this that from which my lord drinketh, and whereby indeed he divineth? Ye have done evil in so doing.'"

Qur'an 12:70
...Then shouted out a crier: "O ye (in) the caravan! Behold! Ye are thieves, without doubt!"

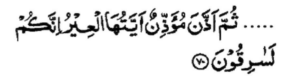

Genesis 44:12
And he searched, and began with the eldest and ended with the youngest; and the cup was found in Benjamin's sack.

Qur'an 12:76
So he began (the search) with their baggage, before (he came to) the baggage of his brother: At length he brought it out of his brother's baggage...

Genesis 44:17

...but the man in whose hand the cup is found, he shall be my servant; and as for you, go up in peace unto your father."

Qur'an 12:75

They said: "The penalty should be that he in whose saddlebag it is found, should be held (as bondman) to atone for the (crime). Thus it is we punish the wrongdoers!"

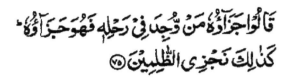

The Life of Moses

His Early Life

Ex. 2:3-12

And when she could no longer hide him, she took for him an ark of bulrushes, and daubed it with slime and with pitch, and put the child therein; and she laid it in the reeds by the river's brink. And his sister stood afar off to learn what would be done to him. And the daughter of Pharaoh came down to wash herself at the river, and her maidens walked along by the riverside; and when she saw the ark among the reeds, she sent her maid to fetch it. And when she had opened it, she saw the child; and behold, the babe wept. And she had compassion on him and said, "This is one of the Hebrews' children."

Qur'an 28:7-9

So We sent this inspiration to the mother of Moses: "Suckle (thy child), but when thou hast fears about him, cast him into the river, but fear not nor grieve: For We shall restore him to thee, and We shall make him one of Our apostles." Then the people of Pharaoh picked him up (from the river). (It was intended) that (Moses) should be to them an adversary and a cause of sorrow: For Pharaoh and Haman and (all) their hosts were men of sin. The wife of Pharaoh said: "(Here is) a joy of the eye, for me and for thee: Slay him not. It may be that he will be of use to us, or we may adopt him as a son." And they perceived not (what they were doing)!

وَأَوْحَيْنَا إِلَىٰٓ أُمِّ مُوسَىٰٓ أَنْ أَرْضِعِيهِ ۖ فَإِذَا خِفْتِ

عَلَيْهِ فَأَلْقِيهِ فِى الْيَمِّ وَلَا تَخَافِى وَلَا تَحْزَنِىٓ ۖ إِنَّا

رَآدُّوهُ إِلَيْكِ وَجَاعِلُوهُ مِنَ الْمُرْسَلِينَ ۝

فَالْتَقَطَهُۥٓ ءَالُ فِرْعَوْنَ لِيَكُونَ لَهُمْ عَدُوًّا وَحَزَنًا ۗ إِنَّ

فِرْعَوْنَ وَهَامَٰنَ وَجُنُودَهُمَا كَانُوا خَٰطِئِينَ ۝

وَقَالَتِ امْرَأَتُ فِرْعَوْنَ قُرَّتُ عَيْنٍ لِّى وَلَكَ ۖ لَا

تَقْتُلُوهُ عَسَىٰٓ أَن يَنفَعَنَآ أَوْ نَتَّخِذَهُۥ وَلَدًا وَهُمْ

لَا يَشْعُرُونَ ۝

Ex. 2:7-10

Then said his sister to Pharaoh's daughter, "Shall I go and call to thee a nurse of the Hebrew women, that she may nurse the child for thee?" And Pharaoh's daughter said to her, "Go." And the maid went and called the child's mother. And Pharaoh's daughter said unto her,

"Take this child away and nurse it for me, and I will give thee thy wages." And the woman took the child, and nursed it. And the child grew, and she brought him unto Pharaoh's daughter, and he became her son. And she called his name Moses that is, Drawn out, and she said, "Because I drew him out of the water."

Qur'an 28:10-13

But there came to be a void in the heart of the mother of Moses: She was going almost to disclose his (case), had We not strengthened her heart (with faith), so that she might remain a (firm) believer. And she said to the sister of (Moses), "Follow him". So she (the sister) watched him in the character of a stranger. And they knew not. And We ordained that he refused suck at first, until (his sister came up and) said: "Shall I point out to you the people of a house that will nourish and bring him up for you and be sincerely attached to him?"...Thus did We restore him to his mother, that her eye might be comforted, that she might not grieve, and that she might know that the promise of Allah is true: But most of them do not understand.

وَأَصْبَحَ فُؤَادُ أُمِّ مُوسَى فَارِغًا إِن كَادَتْ لَتُبْدِى بِهِ
لَوْلَا أَن رَّبَطْنَا عَلَى قَلْبِهَا لِتَكُونَ مِنَ الْمُؤْمِنِينَ ۞
وَقَالَتْ لِأُخْتِهِ قُصِّيهِ فَبَصُرَتْ بِهِ عَن جُنُبٍ وَّ
هُمْ لَا يَشْعُرُونَ ۞
وَحَرَّمْنَا عَلَيْهِ الْمَرَاضِعَ مِن قَبْلُ فَقَالَتْ هَلْ أَدُلُّكُمْ
عَلَى أَهْلِ بَيْتٍ يَكْفُلُونَهُ لَكُمْ وَهُمْ لَهُ نَاصِحُونَ ۞
فَرَدَدْنَاهُ إِلَى أُمِّهِ كَيْ تَقَرَّ عَيْنُهَا وَلَا تَحْزَنَ وَلِتَعْلَمَ أَنَّ
وَعْدَ اللَّهِ حَقٌّ وَلَٰكِنَّ أَكْثَرَهُمْ لَا يَعْلَمُونَ ۞

Ex. 2:11-12

And it came to pass in those days, when Moses was grown, that he went out unto his brethren and looked on their burdens; and he spied an Egyptian smiting a Hebrew, one of his brethren. And he looked this way and that way, and when he saw that there was no man, he slew the Egyptian and hid him in the sand.

Qur'an 28:14-15

When he reached full age, and was firmly established (in life), We bestowed on him wisdom and knowledge: For thus do We reward those who do good. And he entered the City at a time when its people were not watching: And he found there two men fighting, — one of his own religion, and the other, of his foes. Now the man of his own religion appealed to him against his foe, and Moses struck him with his fist and made an end of him. He said: "This is a work of Evil (Satan): For he is an enemy that manifestly misleads!"

وَلَمَّا بَلَغَ أَشُدَّهُ وَاسْتَوَىٰ ءَاتَيْنَٰهُ حُكْمًا وَعِلْمًا وَ
كَذَٰلِكَ نَجْزِى الْمُحْسِنِينَ ۝
وَدَخَلَ الْمَدِينَةَ عَلَىٰ حِينِ غَفْلَةٍ مِّنْ أَهْلِهَا فَوَجَدَ
فِيهَا رَجُلَيْنِ يَقْتَتِلَانِ هَٰذَا مِن شِيعَتِهِ وَهَٰذَا مِنْ
عَدُوِّهِ فَاسْتَغَاثَهُ الَّذِى مِن شِيعَتِهِ عَلَى الَّذِى مِنْ
عَدُوِّهِ فَوَكَزَهُ مُوسَىٰ فَقَضَىٰ عَلَيْهِ قَالَ هَٰذَا مِنْ
عَمَلِ الشَّيْطَٰنِ إِنَّهُ عَدُوٌّ مُّضِلٌّ مُّبِينٌ ۝

Exodus 2:14

And he said, "Who made thee a prince and a judge over us? Intendest thou to kill me as thou killed the Egyptian?" And Moses feared and said, "Surely this thing is known."

Qur'an 28:19

... that man said: "O Moses! Is it thy intention to slay me as thou slewest a man yesterday?..."

قَالَ يَمُوسَىٰ أَتُرِيدُ أَن تَقْتُلَنِى كَمَا قَتَلَتَ

نَفْسًا بِالْأَمْسِ ..... ﷽

God calls Moses

Exodus 3:2

And the angel of the LORD appeared unto him in a flame of fire out of the midst of a bush; and he looked and, behold, the bush burned with fire, and the bush was not consumed.

Qur'an 20:9-10

Has the story of Moses reached thee? Behold, he saw a fire: So he said to his family, "Tarry ye, I perceive a fire; perhaps I can bring you some burning brand therefrom, or find some guidance at the fire."

وَهَلْ أَتَىٰكَ حَدِيثُ مُوسَىٰ ۞

إِذْ رَءَا نَارًا فَقَالَ لِأَهْلِهِ امْكُثُوٓا إِنِّىٓ ءَانَسْتُ نَارًا

لَّعَلِّىٓ ءَاتِيكُم مِّنْهَا بِقَبَسٍ أَوْ أَجِدُ عَلَى النَّارِ هُدًى ۞

Exodus 3:4-5
And when the LORD saw that he turned aside to see, God called unto him out of the midst of the bush and said, "Moses, Moses." And he said, "Here am I." And He said, "Draw not nigh hither. Put off thy shoes from off thy feet, for the place whereon thou standest is holy ground."

Qur'an 20:11-12
But when he came to the fire, a voice was heard: "O Moses! Verily I am thy Lord! Therefore (in My presence) put off thy shoes: Thou art in the sacred valley Tuwa."

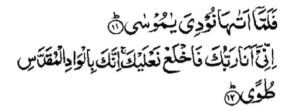

Exodus 4:2-4,6
And the LORD said unto him, "What is that in thine hand?" And he said, "A rod." And He said, "Cast it on the ground." And he cast it on the ground, and it became a serpent; and Moses fled from before it. And the LORD said unto Moses, "Put forth thine hand and take it by the tail." And he put forth his hand and caught it, and it became a rod in his hand— .

Qur'an 20:17-22
"And what is that in thy right hand, O Moses?" He said, "It is my rod: On it I lean; with it I beat down fodder for my flocks; and in it I find other uses." (Allah) said, "Throw it, O Moses!" He threw it, and behold! it was a snake, active in motion. (Allah) said, "Seize it, and fear not: We shall return it at once to its former condition

وَمَا تِلْكَ بِيَمِينِكَ يَٰمُوسَىٰ ۝

قَالَ هِيَ عَصَايَ أَتَوَكَّؤُا عَلَيْهَا وَأَهُشُّ بِهَا

عَلَىٰ غَنَمِي وَلِيَ فِيهَا مَآرِبُ أُخْرَىٰ ۝

قَالَ أَلْقِهَا يَٰمُوسَىٰ ۝

فَأَلْقَاهَا فَإِذَا هِيَ حَيَّةٌ تَسْعَىٰ ۝

قَالَ خُذْهَا وَلَا تَخَفْ سَنُعِيدُهَا سِيرَتَهَا

الْأُولَىٰ ۝

Exodus 4:6
And the LORD said furthermore unto him, "Put now thine hand into thy bosom." And he put his hand into his bosom; and when he took it out, behold, his hand was leprous as snow.

Qur'an 20:22
"Now draw thy hand close to thy side: It shall come forth white (and shining), without harm (or stain). — As another Sign, —

وَاضْمُمْ يَدَكَ إِلَىٰ جَنَاحِكَ تَخْرُجْ بَيْضَآءَ مِنْ

غَيْرِ سُوٓءٍ ءَايَةً أُخْرَىٰ ۝

Exodus 4:10
And Moses said unto the LORD, "O my Lord, I am not eloquent, neither heretofore nor since Thou hast spoken unto Thy servant; but I am slow of speech and of a slow tongue."

Qur'an 20:25-28
(Moses) said: "O my Lord! Expand me my breast; Ease my task for me; And remove the impediment from my speech, So they may understand what I say:..."

قَالَ رَبِّ اشْرَحْ لِي صَدْرِي ۝

وَيَسِّرْ لِي أَمْرِي ۝

وَاحْلُلْ عُقْدَةً مِّن لِّسَانِي ۝

يَفْقَهُوا قَوْلِي ۝

Exodus 4:13-16
And he said, "O my Lord, send, I pray Thee, by the hand of him whom Thou wilt send." And the anger of the LORD was kindled against Moses, and He said, "Is not Aaron the Levite thy brother? I know that he can speak well. And also, behold, he cometh forth to meet thee; and when he seeth thee, he will be glad in his heart. And thou shalt speak unto him and put words in his mouth; and I will be with thy mouth and with his mouth, and will teach you what ye shall do. And he shall be thy spokesman unto the people;

Qur'an 20:29-32
"And give me a Minister from my family Aaron, my brother. Add to my strength through him, and make him share my task:"

وَاجْعَل لِّي وَزِيرًا مِّنْ أَهْلِي ۝

هَارُونَ أَخِي ۝

اشْدُدْ بِهِ أَزْرِي ۝

وَأَشْرِكْهُ فِي أَمْرِي ۝

The Parting Of The Red Sea

Exodus14:16,21,22,23,26
But lift thou up thy rod, and stretch out thine hand over the sea and divide it; and the children of Israel shall go on dry ground through the midst of the sea... And Moses stretched out his hand over the sea; and the LORD caused the sea to go back by a strong east wind all that night and made the sea dry land, and the waters were divided. And the children of Israel went into the midst of the sea upon the dry ground, and the waters were a wall unto them on their right hand and on their left. And the Egyptians pursued, and went in after them to the midst of the sea, even all Pharaoh's horses, his chariots, and his horsemen... And the LORD said unto Moses, "Stretch out thine hand over the sea, that the waters may come again upon the Egyptians, upon their chariots, and upon their horsemen."

Qur'an 26:64-67
Then We told Moses by inspiration: "Strike the sea with thy rod." So it divided, and each separate part became like the huge, firm mass of a mountain. And We made the other party approach thither. We delivered Moses and all who were with him; But We drowned the others.

فَأَوْحَيْنَآ إِلَىٰ مُوسَىٰٓ أَنِ ٱضْرِب بِّعَصَاكَ ٱلْبَحْرَ فَٱنفَلَقَ

فَكَانَ كُلُّ فِرْقٍ كَٱلطَّوْدِ ٱلْعَظِيمِ ۞

وَأَزْلَفْنَا ثَمَّ ٱلْءَاخَرِينَ ۞

وَأَنجَيْنَا مُوسَىٰ وَمَن مَّعَهُۥٓ أَجْمَعِينَ ۞

ثُمَّ أَغْرَقْنَا ٱلْءَاخَرِينَ ۞

The Israelites Complain

Numbers 11:4-5
And the mixed multitude that was among them fell to lusting. And the children of Israel also wept again and said, "Who shall give us flesh to eat? We remember the fish which we ate in Egypt freely, the cucumbers, and the melons, and the leeks, and the onions, and the garlic;

Qur'an 2:61
And remember ye said: "O Moses! We cannot endure one kind of food (always); so beseech thy Lord for us to produce for us of what the earth groweth, — its potherbs, and cucumbers, its garlic, lentils, and onions."

وَإِذْ قُلْتُمْ يَمُوسَى لَن تَصْبِرَ عَلَى طَعَامٍ وَاحِدٍ فَادْعُ

لَنَا رَبَّكَ يُخْرِجْ لَنَا مِمَّا تُنبِتُ الأَرْضُ مِنْ بَقْلِهَا وَ

قِثَّائِهَا وَفُومِهَا وَعَدَسِهَا وَبَصَلِهَا

Purification Sacrifice

Numbers 19:1-2
And the LORD spoke unto Moses and unto Aaron, saying, "This is the ordinance of the law which the LORD hath commanded, saying: 'Speak unto the children of Israel, that they bring thee a red heifer without spot, wherein is no blemish and upon which never came a yoke...'"

Qur'an 2:67-71

And remember Moses said to his people: "Allah commands that ye sacrifice a heifer." They said: "Makest thou a laughingstock of us?" He said: "Allah save me from being an ignorant (fool)!" They said: "Beseech on our behalf thy Lord to make plain to us what (heifer) it is!" He said: "He says: The heifer should be neither too old nor too young, but of middling age: Now do what ye are commanded!" They said: "Beseech on our behalf thy Lord to make plain to us her color." He said: "He says: A fawn-colored heifer, pure and rich in tone, the admiration of beholders!"

وَإِذْ قَالَ مُوسَى لِقَوْمِهِۦٓ إِنَّ ٱللَّهَ يَأْمُرُكُمْ أَن تَذْبَحُوا۟ بَقَرَةً ۖ قَالُوٓا۟ أَتَتَّخِذُنَا هُزُوًا ۖ قَالَ أَعُوذُ بِٱللَّهِ أَنْ أَكُونَ مِنَ ٱلْجَٰهِلِينَ ۝

قَالُوا۟ ٱدْعُ لَنَا رَبَّكَ يُبَيِّن لَّنَا مَا هِىَ ۚ قَالَ إِنَّهُۥ يَقُولُ إِنَّهَا بَقَرَةٌ لَّا فَارِضٌ وَلَا بِكْرٌ عَوَانٌۢ بَيْنَ ذَٰلِكَ ۖ فَٱفْعَلُوا۟ مَا تُؤْمَرُونَ ۝

قَالُوا۟ ٱدْعُ لَنَا رَبَّكَ يُبَيِّن لَّنَا مَا لَوْنُهَا ۚ قَالَ إِنَّهُۥ يَقُولُ إِنَّهَا بَقَرَةٌ صَفْرَآءُ فَاقِعٌ لَّوْنُهَا تَسُرُّ ٱلنَّٰظِرِينَ ۝

Qur'an 2:70-71

They said: "Beseech on our behalf thy Lord to make plain to us what she is: To us are all heifers alike: We wish for guidance, if Allah wills." He said: "He says: A heifer not trained to till the soil or water the fields; sound and without blemish." They said: "Now hast thou brought the truth." Then they offered her in sacrifice but not with goodwill.

قَالُوا ادْعُ لَنَا رَبَّكَ يُبَيِّنْ لَنَا مَا هِيَ إِنَّ الْبَقَرَ تَشَبَهَ
عَلَيْنَا وَإِنَّا إِنْ شَاءَ اللهُ لَمُهْتَدُونَ ۝
قَالَ إِنَّهُ يَقُولُ إِنَّهَا بَقَرَةٌ لَا ذَلُولٌ تُثِيرُ الْأَرْضَ
وَلَا تَسْقِي الْحَرْثَ مُسَلَّمَةٌ لَا شِيَةَ فِيهَا قَالُوا الْـَٰنَ
جِئْتَ بِالْحَقِّ فَذَبَحُوهَا وَمَا كَادُوا يَفْعَلُونَ ۝

Unsolved Murder

Deuteronomy 21:1-4
"If anyone is found slain, lying in the field in the land which the LORD your God is giving you to possess, and it is not known who killed him. Then your elders and judges shall go and measure...And it shall be that the elders of the city nearest to the slain man will take a heifer...and strike off the heifer's neck...."

Qur'an 2:72-73
Remember ye slew a man and fell into a dispute among yourselves as to the crime: But Allah was to bring forth what ye did hide. So We said: "Strike the (body) with a piece of the (heifer)."

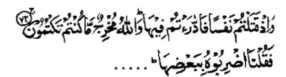

Armies Tried At The Water

Judges 7:4-6
And the LORD said unto Gideon, "The people are yet too many. Bring them down unto the water, and I will

try them for thee there. And it shall be that of whom I say unto thee, `This shall go with thee,' the same shall go with thee; and of whomsoever I say unto thee, `This shall not go with thee,' the same shall not go." So he brought down the people unto the water; and the LORD said unto Gideon, "Every one that lappeth of the water with his tongue as a dog lappeth, him shalt thou set by himself; likewise every one that boweth down upon his knees to drink." And the number of those who lapped, putting their hand to their mouth, was three hundred men; but all the rest of the people bowed down upon their knees to drink water.

Qur'an 2:249
When Talut (Saul) set forth with the armies, he said: "Allah will test you at the stream: If any drinks of its water, he goes not with my army: Only those who taste not of it go with me: A mere sip out of the hand is excused." But they all drank of it, except a few...

فَلَمَّا فَصَلَ طَالُوتُ بِالْجُنُودِ قَالَ إِنَّ اللّهَ مُبْتَلِيكُم بِنَهَرٍ فَمَن شَرِبَ مِنْهُ فَلَيْسَ مِنِّي وَمَن لَّمْ يَطْعَمْهُ فَإِنَّهُ مِنِّي إِلَّا مَنِ اغْتَرَفَ غُرْفَةً بِيَدِهِ فَشَرِبُوا مِنْهُ إِلَّا قَلِيلًا مِّنْهُمْ .....

God Convicts David

2 Sam 12:1-13
And the LORD sent Nathan unto David. And he came unto him, and said unto him, "There were two men in

one city, the one rich and the other poor. The rich man had exceeding many flocks and herds. But the poor man had nothing, save one little ewe lamb, which he had bought and nourished up. And it grew up together with him and with his children... And there came a traveller unto the rich man, and he was unwilling to take of his own flock and of his own herd to dress for the wayfaring man who had come unto him, but took the poor man's lamb and dressed it for the man who had come to him." And David's anger was greatly kindled against the man, and he said to Nathan, "As the LORD liveth, the man who hath done this thing shall surely die. And he shall restore the lamb fourfold... And Nathan said to David, "Thou art the man..." And David said unto Nathan, "I have sinned against the LORD." And Nathan said unto David, "The LORD also hath put away thy sin; thou shalt not die."

Qur'an 38:21-24

Has the Story of the Disputants reached thee? Behold, they climbed over the wall of the private chamber; When they entered the presence of David, and he was terrified of them, they said: "Fear not: We are two disputants, one of whom has wronged the other: Decide now between us with truth, and treat us not with unjustice, but guide us to the even Path. . "This man is my brother: He has nine and ninety ewes, and I have (but) one: Yet he says, `Commit her to my care,' and is (moreover) harsh to me in speech." (David) said: "He has undoubtedly wronged thee in demanding thy (single) ewe to be added to his (flock of) ewes:... And David gathered that We had tried him: He asked forgiveness of his Lord, fell down, bowing (in prostration), and turned (to Allah in repentance).

قَالَ لَقَدْ ظَلَمَكَ بِسُؤَالِ نَعْجَتِكَ إِلَى نِعَاجِهِ

وَإِنَّ كَثِيرًا مِنَ الْخُلَطَاءِ لَيَبْغِي بَعْضُهُمْ عَلَى

بَعْضٍ إِلَّا الَّذِينَ آمَنُوا وَعَمِلُوا الصَّالِحَاتِ وَ

قَلِيلٌ مَا هُمْ وَظَنَّ دَاوُدُ أَنَّمَا فَتَنَّاهُ فَاسْتَغْفَرَ

رَبَّهُ وَخَرَّ رَاكِعًا وَأَنَابَ ۩

وَهَلْ أَتَاكَ نَبَأُ الْخَصْمِ إِذْ تَسَوَّرُوا الْمِحْرَابَ

إِذْ دَخَلُوا عَلَى دَاوُدَ فَفَزِعَ مِنْهُمْ قَالُوا لَا تَخَفْ

خَصْمَانِ بَغَى بَعْضُنَا عَلَى بَعْضٍ فَاحْكُمْ بَيْنَنَا

بِالْحَقِّ وَلَا تُشْطِطْ وَاهْدِنَا إِلَى سَوَاءِ الصِّرَاطِ

إِنَّ هَذَا أَخِي لَهُ تِسْعٌ وَتِسْعُونَ نَعْجَةً وَلِيَ

نَعْجَةٌ وَاحِدَةٌ فَقَالَ أَكْفِلْنِيهَا وَعَزَّنِي

فِي الْخِطَابِ ۞

King Solomon And The Queen Of Sheba

1 Kings 10:1

And when the queen of Sheba heard of the fame of Solomon concerning the name of the LORD, she came to test him with hard questions.

Qur'an 27:23
"I found (there) a woman ruling over them and provided with every requisite, and she has a magnificent throne.

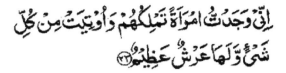

1 Kings 10:10
And she gave the king a hundred and twenty talents of gold, and of spices a very great store, and precious stones; there came no more such abundance of spices as these which the queen of Sheba gave to King Solomon.

Qur'an 27:35-36
"But I am going to send him a present, and (wait) to see with what (answer) return (my) ambassadors." Now when (the embassy) came to Solomon, he said: "Will ye give me abundance in wealth?...

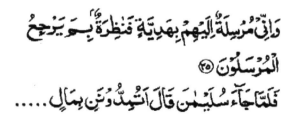

Elijah Confronts The Prophets Of Baal

1 Kings 18:21
And Elijah came unto all the people and said, "How long halt ye between two opinions? If the LORD be God, follow Him; but if Baal, then follow him." And the people answered him not a word.

Qur'an 37:123-125
So also was Elias among those sent (by Us). Behold, he said to his people, "Will ye not fear (Allah)?"Will ye call upon Baal and forsake the Best of Creators, –

وَإِنَّ إِلْيَاسَ لَمِنَ الْمُرْسَلِينَ ۝

إِذْ قَالَ لِقَوْمِهِ أَلَا تَتَّقُونَ ۝

أَتَدْعُونَ بَعْلًا وَتَذَرُونَ أَحْسَنَ الْخَالِقِينَ ۝

Job - God's Servant

Job 1:1,
There was a man in the land of Uz, whose name was Job; and that man was perfect and upright, and one who feared God and eschewed evil......Also the LORD gave Job twice as much as he had before.... So the LORD blessed the latter end of Job more than his beginning;

Qur'an 38:41,43
Commemorate Our Servant Job... And We gave him (back) his people, and doubled their number, – as a Grace from Ourselves, and a thing for commemoration, for all who have Understanding.

وَاذْكُرْ عَبْدَنَا أَيُّوبَ ......

وَوَهَبْنَا لَهُ أَهْلَهُ وَمِثْلَهُم مَّعَهُمْ رَحْمَةً مِّنَّا وَ

ذِكْرَىٰ لِأُولِى الْأَلْبَابِ ۝

Gog and Magog

Ezekiel 38:1-3

And the word of the LORD came unto me, saying, "Son of man, set thy face against Gog, the land of Magog, the chief prince of Meshech and Tubal, and prophesy against him and say, `Thus saith the Lord GOD: Behold, I am against thee, O Gog, the chief prince of Meshech and Tubal.

Qur'an 18:93-94

Until, when he reached (a tract) between two mountains, he found, beneath them, a people who scarcely understood a word. They said: "O Zulqarnain! The Gog and Magog (people) do great mischief on earth...

حَتَّىٰٓ إِذَا بَلَغَ بَيْنَ ٱلسَّدَّيْنِ وَجَدَ مِن دُونِهِمَا

قَوْمًا لَّا يَكَادُونَ يَفْقَهُونَ قَوْلًا ۝

قَالُوا يَـٰذَا ٱلْقَرْنَيْنِ إِنَّ يَأْجُوجَ وَمَأْجُوجَ مُفْسِدُونَ

فِى ٱلْأَرْضِ .....

Jonah Flees From God

Jonah 1:1-4

Now the word of the LORD came unto Jonah the son of Amittai, saying, "Arise, go to Nineveh, that great city, and cry out against it; for their wickedness has come up before Me." But Jonah rose up to flee unto Tarshish from the presence of the LORD; and he went down to Joppa, and found a ship going to Tarshish. So he paid the fare thereof, and went down into it to go with them unto Tarshish from the presence of the LORD. But the LORD sent out a great wind into the sea, and there was a mighty tempest in the sea, so that the ship was likely to be broken.

Qur'an 37:139-140
So also was Jonah among those sent (by Us). When he ran away (like a slave from captivity) to the ship (fully) laden,

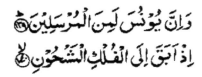

Jonah Swallowed By The Big Fish

Jonah 1:7, 11, 12, 15,17
And they said every one to his fellow, "Come, and let us cast lots, that we may know for whose cause this evil is upon us." So they cast lots, and the lot fell upon Jonah... hen said they unto him, "What shall we do unto thee, that the sea may be calm unto us?" For the sea grew more and more tempestuous. And he said unto them, "Take me up and cast me forth into the sea. So shall the sea be calm unto you, for I know that for my sake this great tempest is upon you."... So they took up Jonah and cast him forth into the sea, and the sea ceased from her raging... Now the LORD had prepared a great fish to swallow up Jonah. And Jonah was in the belly of the fish three days and three nights.

Qur'an 37:141-142
He (agreed to) cast lots, and he was condemned: Then the big Fish did swallow him, and he had done acts worthy of blame

فَمَا هُوَ فَكَانَ مِنَ الْمُدْحَضِينَ ۞

فَالْتَقَمَهُ الْحُوتُ وَهُوَمُلِيمٌ ۞

Jonah 2:1-2,10

Then Jonah prayed unto the LORD his God out of the fish's belly, and said: "I cried by reason of mine affliction unto the LORD, and He heard me. Out of the belly of hell cried I, and Thou heardest my voice... And the LORD spoke unto the fish, and it vomited out Jonah upon the dry land.

Qur'an 37:143-145

Had it not been that he (repented and) glorified Allah, He would certainly have remained inside the Fish till the Day of Resurrection.

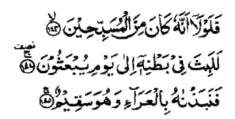

فَلَوْلَا أَنَّهُ كَانَ مِنَ الْمُسَبِّحِينَ ۞

لَلَبِثَ فِي بَطْنِهِ إِلَى يَوْمِ يُبْعَثُونَ ۞

فَنَبَذْنَاهُ بِالْعَرَاءِ وَهُوَسَقِيمٌ ۞

Jonah Enters Nineveh

Jonah 3:1-3

And the word of the LORD came unto Jonah the second time, saying, "Arise, go unto Nineveh, that great city, and preach unto it the preaching that I bid thee." So Jonah arose and went unto Nineveh, according to the word of the LORD. Now Nineveh was an exceeding great city of three days' journey.

Qur'an 37:147
And We sent him (on a mission) to a hundred thousand (men) or more.

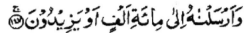

Jonah 3:5,10
So the people of Nineveh believed God, and proclaimed a fast and put on sackcloth, from the greatest of them even to the least of them... And God saw their works, that they turned from their evil way. And God repented of the evil that He had said that He would do unto them, and He did it not.

Qur'an 37:148
And they believed; so We permitted them to enjoy (their life) for a while.

فَآمَنُوا فَمَتَّعْنَـٰهُمْ إِلَىٰ حِينٍ ۝

Jonah Under The Gourd

Jonah 4:6
And the LORD God prepared a gourd, and made it to come up over Jonah, that it might be a shadow over his head to deliver him from his grief. So Jonah was exceeding glad for the gourd.

Qur'an 37:146
And We caused to grow over him, a spreading plant of the Gourd kind.

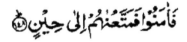

New Testament Accounts

The Birth Of John The Baptist

Luke 1:13
But the angel said unto him, "Fear not, Zacharias, for thy prayer is heard, and thy wife Elizabeth shall bear thee a son, and thou shalt call his name John.

Qur'an 19:7
(His prayer was answered): "O Zakariya! We give thee good news of a son: His name shall be Yahya (John)."

Luke 1:18
And Zacharias said unto the angel, "Whereby shall I know this? For I am an old man, and my wife well stricken in years."

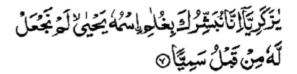

Qur'an 19:8
He said: "O my Lord! How shall I have a son, when my wife is barren and I have grown quite decrepit from old age?"

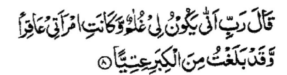

Luke 1:20
And behold, thou shalt be dumb and not able to speak until the day that these things shall be performed,

because thou believest not my words which shall be fulfilled in their season."

Qur'an 19:10

(Zakariya) said: "O my Lord! Give me a Sign." "Thy Sign,"
was the answer, "Shall be that thou shalt speak to no man for
three nights, although thou art not dumb."

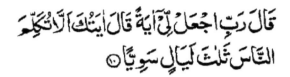

Luke 1:21,22

And the people waited for Zacharias, and marvelled that he tarried so long in the temple. And when he came out, he could not speak unto them, and they perceived that he had seen a vision in the temple; for he beckoned unto them and remained speechless.

Qur'an 19:11

So Zakariya came out to his people from his chamber: He told
them by signs to celebrate Allah's praises in the morning
and in the evening.

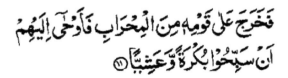

The Birth Of Jesus

Luke 1:28

And the angel came in unto her (Mary)...

Qur'an 19:17

...then We sent to her (Mary) Our angel, and he appeared before her as a man in all respects.

Luke 1:30-31

And the angel said unto her, "Fear not, Mary, for thou hast found favour with God. And behold, thou shalt conceive in thy womb and bring forth a Son, and shalt call His name Jesus.

Qur'an 3:45

Behold! The angels said: "O Mary! Allah giveth thee glad tidings of a Word from Him: His name will be Christ Jesus, the son of Mary, held in honor in this world and the Hereafter and of (the company of) those nearest to Allah;"

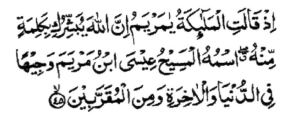

Luke 1:34

Then said Mary unto the angel, "How shall this be, seeing I know not a man?"

Qur'an 19:20

She said: "How shall I have a son, seeing that no man has touched me, and I am not Unchaste?"

قَالَتْ أَنَّى يَكُونُ لِى غُلَٰمٌ وَلَمْ يَمْسَسْنِى بَشَرٌ وَلَمْ

Jesus - The Prophet

Matt 5:17
"Think not that I am come to destroy the Law or the Prophets. I am not come to destroy, but to fulfil.

Qur'an 3:50
"(I have come to you), to attest the Law which was before me.

وَمُصَدِّقًا لِّمَا بَيْنَ يَدَىَّ مِنَ التَّوْرَىٰةِ

Matthew 15:24
But He answered and said, "I am not sent but unto the lost sheep of the house of Israel."

Qur'an 3:49
And (appoint him) an apostle to the children of Israel

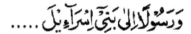 ..... وَرَسُولًا إِلَىٰ بَنِىٓ إِسْرَآءِيلَ

Jesus - The Word

John 1:1,14
In the beginning was the **Word,** and the **Word** was with God ...and the **Word** was made flesh...

Qur'an 3:39,45
"Allah doth give thee glad tidings of Yahya, witnessing the truth of a Word from Allah... Behold! The angels said: "O Mary! Allah giveth thee glad tidings of a Word from Him: His name will be Christ Jesus, the son of Mary, held in honor

in this world and the Hereafter and of (the company of) those
nearest to Allah;"

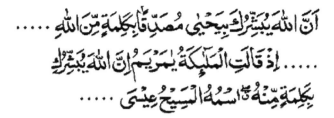

The Ascension Of Jesus

Acts 1:11
...this same Jesus which is taken up from you into
heaven...

Qur'an 4:158
Nay, God raised him (Jesus) up unto Himself.

بَلْ رَّفَعَهُ اللّهُ إِلَيْهِ .....

The Sinfulness Of Mankind

Romans 3:23
For all have sinned, and come short of the glory of God.

Qur'an 35:45
If Allah were to punish men according to what they deserve,
He would not leave on the back of the (earth) a single living
creature:

وَلَوْ يُؤَاخِذُ اللّهُ النَّاسَ بِمَا كَسَبُوا مَا تَرَكَ عَلَى

ظَهْرِهَا مِنْ دَآبَّةٍ .....

Gal 6:5

For every man shall bear his own burden

Qur'an 53:38

Namely, that no bearer of burdens can bear the burden of another;

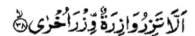

Jesus Is Above All

Ephesians 1:20-21

...which he wrought in Christ when He raised Him from the dead and set Him at His own right hand in the heavenly places, far above all principality and power and might and dominion, and every name that is named, not only in this world, but also in that which is to come.

Qur'an 3:45

Behold! The angels said: "O Mary! Allah giveth thee glad tidings of a Word from Him: His name will be Christ Jesus, the son of Mary, held in honor in this world and the Hereafter and of (the company of) those nearest to Allah,"

إِذْ قَالَتِ الْمَلَٰٓئِكَةُ يَٰمَرْيَمُ إِنَّ اللَّهَ يُبَشِّرُكِ بِكَلِمَةٍ

مِّنْهُ ٱسْمُهُ الْمَسِيحُ عِيسَى ابْنُ مَرْيَمَ وَجِيهًا

فِى الدُّنْيَا وَالْأَخِرَةِ وَمِنَ الْمُقَرَّبِينَ ۝

Heavenly Joy

Rev. 21:3-4
And I heard a great voice out of Heaven, saying, "Behold, the tabernacle of God is with men, and He will dwell with them; and they shall be His people, and God Himself shall be with them and be their God. And God shall wipe away all tears from their eyes, and there shall be no more death, neither sorrow, nor crying, neither shall there be any more pain; for the former things are passed away."

Qur'an 37:58-59
Is it (the case) that we shall not die, "Except our first death, and that we shall not be punished?"

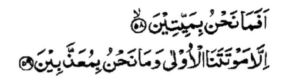

What Do You Think About These "Revelations"?

The Prophet married Zainab

Zaid, son of Haritha, was a freedman and adopted son of the Prophet. The Prophet gave his own cousin Zainab, daughter of Jahsh, in marriage to Zaid eight years before the Hijrah.

In Islam, marriage is lawfully contracted when based on the consent of both partners. Therefore, we cannot assume that the Prophet forced his cousin Zainab to marry

Zaid even though Zainab was a high-born while Zaid was a freedman.

In the course of time, there arose a misunderstanding as is normal in most marriages, and the Prophet Muhammad happened to be the arbitrator over the conflict.

According to the Qur'an, Allah gave a message to the Prophet to disclose during the arbitration. Prior to this, Allah had commanded Muhammad to fear Him and only Him alone:

Qur'an 33:1
O Prophet fear Allah…

Surprisingly, instead of heeding to the command of Allah, the Prophet feared the people and therefore hid the message that was to be disclosed. However, finally the marriage between Zaid and Zainab was broken under the auspices of the Prophet. Before long, Zainab became the wife of the Prophet, supposedly under the command of Allah and as an example for others who may want to marry the wives of their adopted sons. All this is recorded in the Qur'an:

Qur'an 33:37
Behold! Thou didst say to one who had received the grace of Allah and thy favor: "Retain thou (in wedlock) thy wife, and fear Allah." But thou didst hide in thy heart that which Allah was about to make manifest: Thou didst fear the people, but it is more fitting that thou shouldst fear Allah. Then when Zaid had dissolved (his marriage) with her, with the necessary (formality), We joined her in marriage to thee: In order that (in future) there may be no difficulty to the Believers in (the matter of) marriage with the wives of their adopted sons, when the latter have dissolved with

the necessary (formality) (their marriage) with them. And
Allah's command must be fulfilled.

وَإِذْ تَقُولُ لِلَّذِي أَنْعَمَ اللَّهُ عَلَيْهِ وَأَنْعَمْتَ عَلَيْهِ
أَمْسِكْ عَلَيْكَ زَوْجَكَ وَاتَّقِ اللَّهَ وَتُخْفِي فِي نَفْسِكَ
مَا اللَّهُ مُبْدِيهِ وَتَخْشَى النَّاسَ وَاللَّهُ أَحَقُّ أَن تَخْشَاهُ
فَلَمَّا قَضَى زَيْدٌ مِّنْهَا وَطَرًا زَوَّجْنَاكَهَا لِكَيْ لَا يَكُونَ
عَلَى الْمُؤْمِنِينَ حَرَجٌ فِي أَزْوَاجِ أَدْعِيَائِهِمْ إِذَا قَضَوْا
مِنْهُنَّ وَطَرًا وَكَانَ أَمْرُ اللَّهِ مَفْعُولًا ۝

This account is supposed to be one of the revealed messages of Allah to the Prophet. Assuming Zaid and Zainab and all others who were witnesses to this incident were alive now; would they accept the fact that this portion of the Qur'an was actually **revealed** to the Prophet? Was it revealed to the Prophet Muhammad before, after or during the course of the incident?

Oath Taking

Whoever wants to take an oath does so by swearing by something that is greater than himself. As we all know, Allah is the greatest of all. He is far above all His creation. Yet, astonishingly, in the Qur'an we find Allah swearing by the Fig tree, the Olive, Mount Sinai and a City as recorded in Sura 95 and many other places. You can search through and find other examples for yourself.

Jesus the Son of God

The accounts by Luke about the births of John the Baptist (Yahya) and Jesus have also appeared in the Qur'an; hence Luke's account must be authentic if the Qur'an is considered authentic. Luke recorded that Jesus had no human father, but was conceived in a virgin by the Holy Spirit (Luke. 1:35). The Qur'an also reveals the same fact (Qur'an 21:91)

Luke recorded that it was because of the above truth, that Jesus was called the "Son of God." How do you then consider the "revelation" to Muhammad to the effect that; if the Christians say Jesus is the Son of God, Allah's curse would be upon them? (Qur'an 9:30)

In fact, according to Luke, it was not Christians who first said that Jesus was the Son of God but rather, it was the Angel Gabriel. He explained to Mary that since her child, who was to be named Jesus, would be conceived through the Holy Spirit, therefore he would be called the Son of God. .

Did Allah then forget His own declaration centuries later, and send the same Angel Gabriel to the Prophet of Islam with such a contradictory message? How does Allah reveal His messages?

He frowned and turned away

The Prophet of Islam was once deeply and earnestly engaged in trying to persuade one of the great Quraysh leaders of the truth of Islam when he was interrupted by a poor blind man; called Abdullah Ibn Ummi Maktum, who also wanted to learn the faith. According to Qur'an chapter 80:1-2 the Prophet's response was to frown and turn away. This incident took place in the presence of many witnesses.

The question is, why was it recorded in the Qur'an when the Qur'an is said to be revelation. How could it be explained to these pagan Quraysh leaders, and would they accept it, that this incident was **revealed** to the prophet? When was it revealed – was it before or after or during the course of the incident?

Jerusalem as the Qibla

In the early days, before the Prophet and his followers were organised as a people, they followed the practice of the Jews by turning their faces towards Jerusalem when they prayed. Did Allah permit the Prophet to turn to Jerusalem in view of the sacred city of Mecca? Does this mean that it is true that Allah has favoured and raised the Israelites above all nations and for that matter, is Jerusalem exalted above all cities in the sight of Allah? (Qur'an 2:47; 2:122; 45:16)

As long as the Jews remained calm and offered no opposition, the sacred city of Jerusalem remained the Qibla for the Prophet and his followers. Was it because Allah told the Prophet to copy the earlier prophets, that he copied the Jewish practice of turning to Jerusalem to pray?

> *Qur'an 6:90*
> *"Those were the prophets who received God's guidance. Copy the guidance they received..."*

When despised and persecuted, the Prophet and his followers migrated to Medina, hoping that they would be welcome there. Muhammad presented himself as the Prophet that the Jews were expecting. However, unfortunately for him, their scriptures did not point to the advent of an Arab prophet of Islam. The Jews were rather waiting for the Prophet whose coming was foretold by Moses who would be a Jew and their Messiah. They believed that when he came, the Jews would once more become a great nation with a king like David who would rule over all the other nations. Therefore they could not accept Muhammad.

For those willing to see, Jesus revealed that he was the long-awaited Messiah and Prophet. How could there be another prophet to fulfil the Torah when Jesus had already come to do just that?

Qur'an 61:6

"And remember Jesus the Son of Mary said; O children of Israel! I am the apostle of Allah sent to you to confirm (fulfil) the Torah, which came before me..."

Over five hundred years before the birth of Muhammad, Jesus had already declared this truth in the following words:

John 5:39

"Search the Scriptures, for in them ye think ye have eternal life; and it is they which testify of Me."

John 5: 46

"If you believed Moses, you would believe me, for he wrote about me."

Matthew 5:17

"Think not that I am come to destroy the Law or the Prophets. I am not come to destroy, but to fulfill."

Since Muhammad was an Arab and not a Jew, the Jews could not accept Muhammad as the Prophet they were expecting and therefore they opposed him and his followers. As a result, the Prophet became extremely offended and began to look for another more pleasing direction to turn to in prayer. Allah saw him at this point and intervened:

Qur'an 2:144
We see the turning of thy face (for guidance) to the heavens:
Now shall We turn thee to a Qibla that shall please thee. Turn
then thy face in the direction of sacred Mosque: Wherever ye
are, turn your faces in that direction. The people of the Book
know well that is the truth from their Lord. Nor is Allah
unmindful of what they do.

قَدْ نَرَىٰ تَقَلُّبَ وَجْهِكَ فِى السَّمَاءِ فَلَنُوَلِّيَنَّكَ
قِبْلَةً تَرْضَاهَا ۚ فَوَلِّ وَجْهَكَ شَطْرَ الْمَسْجِدِ الْحَرَامِ
وَحَيْثُ مَا كُنْتُمْ فَوَلُّوا وُجُوهَكُمْ شَطْرَهُ ۗ وَإِنَّ
الَّذِينَ أُوتُوا الْكِتَٰبَ لَيَعْلَمُونَ أَنَّهُ الْحَقُّ مِنْ رَبِّهِمْ ۗ
وَمَا اللَّهُ بِغَٰفِلٍ عَمَّا يَعْمَلُونَ ۝

Don't you know the Prophet was an Arab and would
automatically turn to his native city of Mecca once he
rejected the Jewish Qibla?

Conclusion

When we look at all the evidence presented, we are left
with the following questions:

a. Did Allah reveal His mind and purpose to Muhammad
    but fail to disclose it to the earlier prophets?
b. Is there any truth (not distorted truth) recorded in the
    Qur'an that was not first recorded in the Bible written
    centuries before the birth of Muhammad?
c. It is claimed that the Qur'an contains prophecies of
    which, some have been fulfilled while others are yet to

be fulfilled. Are there any such prophecies that cannot be traced back to the Bible?

d. What then is the need for the Qur'an if its content (excluding distorted truths) can be found in the Bible? Can we find anything **new** that has been **revealed** by Allah?

The only fresh revelation appears to be that which kicks against the truths of the Bible like:

1. The Qur'an implies that it was Ishmael whom Abraham was commanded to offer as a sacrifice to God (Qur'an 37:99-133; Qur'an 11:71), whereas the Bible specifically names Isaac as the one whom Abraham is to sacrifice. (Genesis 22:2).

2. The Qur'an claims that one of Noah's sons was drowned in the flood (Qur'an 11:25-48), whereas the Bible declares that all three sons and their wives were saved in the ark (Genesis 5:32; 7:7,13).

3. In the Qur'an, Zechariah, the father of John the Baptist (Yahya), became dumb for only three days (Qur'an 3:41), whereas the Bible reveals that he remained dumb until after the child was born and named, a period of at least nine months (Luke 1:18-20, 23-24, 63-64).

4   The Qur'an denies the crucifixion of Jesus (Qur'an 4:157), whereas in the Bible, it is prophesied in the Old Testament (for example, Psalm 22, Isaiah 53; Zechariah 12:10) and confirmed in many places throughout the New Testament (for example, Matthew 27:27-44; John 19:18; Acts 2:36; Galations 3:10).

4. According to the Qur'an, Allah's curse will come upon anyone who declares that Jesus is the Son of God (Qur'an 9:30). However, in the Bible, it was the Angel Gabriel who first disclosed to Mary that Jesus is the Son of God (Luke 1:35). Is the Angel Gabriel then also

cursed? Was it not God himself who gave the angel the words to say? How many angels bear the name Gabriel? Are there more than one?

We do well to pay attention to Paul's warning:

Galatians 1:8-9
But though we or an angel from heaven preach any other gospel unto you than that which we have preached unto you, let him be accursed. As we said before, so I say now again, if any man preach any other gospel unto you than that ye have received, let him be accursed.

1. The Qur'an denies the doctrine of the Trinity (Qur'an 4:171; 5:75-76, 119-120), although at the same time it misrepresents it as "The Father, the Son and the Mother" (Qur'an 5:119). However, it was Jesus himself who presented it as "The Father, the Son and the Holy Spirit," while the apostles also preached it. (Matthew 28:19).
2. In the Qur'an, the child Moses was adopted by the wife of Pharaoh (Qur'an 28:9), whereas in the Bible, it was the daughter of Pharaoh who adopted Moses (Exodus 2:10).

We must conclude that if Luke was able to write (around AD 60) certain accounts, which also appear in the Qur'an and which were supposedly **revealed** to Muhammad after AD 610, Luke must have been a super-prophet!

Not only that, but if the Qur'an and its compilation is considered a miracle, even though all the scribes wrote while surrounding the Prophet at one place, then the Bible and its compilation is far beyond description. For the Bible contains 66 books, written over a period of more than 1,500 years by about 40 different prophets, apostles and teachers who were separated both by distance and time and mostly unknown to each other.

It can only be by divine inspiration that these writers all wrote with one basic theme – the redemption of mankind through Jesus, the Messiah, God's Son, Saviour of the world and Lord of all. The Old Testament was looking forward to his coming, everything in the New Testament points to his life, death resurrection and exaltation as the source of human salvation, power and joy.

The Bible therefore still stands valid and authentic; complete as the true light for human salvation here in this life and in the hereafter. The transforming power of the Bible is still fresh and potent to change lives and restore newness, hope, confidence, love and power.

The Bible was indeed inspired by God Himself as His own word. Therefore as the word of God it cannot be dismissed or ignored but has a vital role to fulfil in the perfecting of God's people.

2 Timothy 3:16-17
All Scripture is given by inspiration of God and is profitable for doctrine, for reproof, for correction, for instruction in righteousness, that the man of God may be perfect, thoroughly equipped for all good works.

In the light of what we have shared in this chapter we leave the reader with the following question to consider:
What then is true revelation?

3

SHOW US THE STRAIGHT WAY

Introduction

Muslims are guided by six articles of faith that bind them to believe in all the prophets. This means that they claim to believe in Abraham, Jacob, Isaac, Noah, Muhammad and also Jesus as prophets of equal status. At the mention of Jesus' name, Muslims say: *Alaihim Wasalam*, meaning: "May peace be upon Him."

Clearly, Muslims have respect for Jesus. They also believe in some of the facts about Jesus such as his Second Coming. However, it is tragic that Muslims reject the essential aspect of Jesus' identity and his real mission to this world. In particular, Muslims do not believe in the **Sonship** of Jesus Christ and nor do they believe in the cleansing power of his blood. They do not accept the fact that it is only through Jesus that salvation can be obtained.

The Qur'an however provides a lot of amazing facts about Jesus that should prompt Muslims to examine critically and to review their present beliefs about Jesus. As we shall see from the Qur'anic passages treated below, the few facts Muslims accept about Jesus are just a fraction of what the Qur'an reveals about Him.

Mercy

Mercy is one of the ninety-nine (99) names or attributes that Muslims have for Allah. Apart from Sura Taubah (Sura 9), every Qur'anic chapter begins with the words: *Bismillahi Rahmani Rahim* -"In the name of Allah, the Gracious, the Merciful." By this, Muslims recognise Allah as the most merciful and most gracious.

At a point in time, people of the Qur'anic age must have recognised the limitations of justification through religious practices and asked Allah to bestow mercy on them from Himself:

> *Sura Imran 3:8*
> *"Our Lord!" (They say), "Let not our hearts deviate now after Thou hast guided us, but grant us mercy from Thine own Presence; for Thou art the Grantor of bounties without measure."*

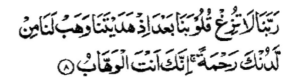

Six centuries after Jesus Christ had completed all the work of salvation, these people were asking Allah for what had already been accomplished. And Allah referred them to what had transpired between Mary and the angel Gabriel:

Sura Margam 19: 22
He said: "So (it will be): Thy Lord saith, 'That is easy for
Me: And (We wish) to appoint him as a Sign unto men and
a Mercy from Us.' It is a matter (so) decreed."

قَالَ كَذَلِكِ قَالَ رَبُّكِ هُوَ عَلَيَّ هَيِّنٌ وَلِنَجْعَلَهُ ءَايَةً
لِلنَّاسِ وَرَحْمَةً مِّنَّا وَكَانَ أَمْرًا مَّقْضِيًّا ﴿٢﴾

These were the words that the Angel Gabriel gave
Mary when she asked him how she could bring forth when
no man had touched her. In the response, the Qur'an states
that Allah made Jesus the "**Mercy**" from Himself as well
as a "Sign unto men." However, Muslims say that Jesus
came only for the Israelites and not for all men. Have they
forgotten or are they unaware that Jesus also ministered to
non-Jews and that he ordered his disciples to preach the
gospel to **all** nations (Matthew 28:19)?

The Way

Sura Fatihah 1:6 reads: *Ihidinaa Siraata mustaquima.*

This short verse has different interpretations because it
is of keen interest. Here are some of these interpretations:

- *Guide us in the right path.* (Maulawi Sher-Ali)
- *Guide us along the right path.* (Muhammad Zafrulla Khan)
- *Guide us to the straight path.* (Mahmud Y. Zahid)
- *Show us the straight path.* (Pickthall)
- *Show us the straight way.* (Yusuf Ali)

Combining these different translations, we can express the verse as:

Guide us to and in the Straight Way.

No matter which translation is chosen, one fact is clear and that is that Muslims are still asking for the way. However, the Qur'an itself reveals more to us about the Straight Way and provides some facts that can help the sincere Muslim to find it. Consider the following:

Qur'an 4:176
Then those who believe in Allah, and hold fast to Him, --soon will He admit them to Mercy and Grace from Himself, and guide them to Himself by a straight Way.

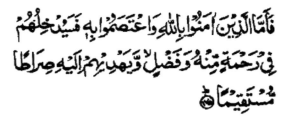

This verse tells us clearly that those who believe in Allah and depend on Him will be admitted into the fold of Allah's Mercy. As we have already seen, Allah's Mercy is Jesus and it is also he who will guide them on a straight path to Allah.

When Muhammad was questioned by some of the believers about the future destiny of his followers, he was told to give the following reply:

Qur'an 46:9
Say: "I am no bringer of newfangled doctrine among the apostles, nor do I know what will be done with me or with

you. I follow but that which is revealed to me by inspiration;
I am but a Warner open and clear."

قُل مَا كُنتُ بِدْعًا مِّنَ ٱلرُّسُلِ وَمَآ أَدْرِى مَا يُفْعَلُ
بِن وَلَا بِكُمْ إِنْ أَتَّبِعُ إِلَّا مَا يُوحَىٰ إِلَىَّ وَمَآ أَنَا إِلَّا
نَذِيرٌ مُّبِينٌ ۝

In contrast, the following prophecy was revealed about Jesus before his birth:

Qur'an 3:45
Behold! The angels said: "O Mary! Allah giveth thee glad
tidings of a Word from Him: His name will be Christ Jesus,
the son of Mary, held in honor in this world and the Hereafter
and of (the company of) those nearest to Allah;"

إِذْ قَالَتِ ٱلْمَلَٰٓئِكَةُ يَٰمَرْيَمُ إِنَّ ٱللَّهَ يُبَشِّرُكِ بِكَلِمَةٍ
مِّنْهُ ٱسْمُهُ ٱلْمَسِيحُ عِيسَى ٱبْنُ مَرْيَمَ وَجِيهًا
فِى ٱلدُّنْيَا وَٱلْءَاخِرَةِ وَمِنَ ٱلْمُقَرَّبِينَ ۝

The Qur'an also says that the followers of Jesus will be placed above those who disbelieve until the Day of Resurrection (see Qur'an 3:55).

We must realise that we need to follow someone who is honoured in this world and in the hereafter if we are to walk along the straight path of God. No wonder, when Thomas asked Jesus about the way, Jesus replied:

John 14:6
"I am the way, the truth and the life. No-one comes to the Father except through me."

Love

The Qur'an emphasises the fact that Christians love Muslims:

Qur'an 5:85
Strongest among men in enmity to the Believers wilt thou find the Jews and Pagans; and in nearest among them in love to the Believers wilt thou find those who say, "we are Christians." Because among them are men devoted to learning and men who have renounced the world and they are not arrogant.

لَتَجِدَنَّ اَشَدَّالنَّاسِ عَدَاوَةًۭ لِّلَّذِيۡنَ اٰمَنُواالۡيَهُوۡدَ وَالَّذِيۡنَ اَشۡرَكُوۡا ۚ وَلَتَجِدَنَّ اَقۡرَبَهُمۡ مَّوَدَّةًۭ لِّلَّذِيۡنَ اٰمَنُواالَّذِيۡنَ قَالُوۡۤاِنَّاَنَصٰرَىٰ ۚ ذٰلِكَ بِاَنَّ مِنۡهُمۡ قِسِّيۡسِيۡنَ وَرُهۡبَانًاوَّاَنَّهُمۡ لَايَسۡتَكۡبِرُوۡنَ ۞

In Muhammad's time, there were followers of Jesus who had completely renounced the world and were not proud but rather they were known for their love. Indeed, when Muhammad's own followers were persecuted in Mecca, Muhammad was so confident in the love of Christians that he directed his followers to flee to a Christian king, called King Negus of Abyssinia (present-day Ethiopia). Some of the Meccans pursued the Muslims to Abyssinia in order to capture them, but this Christian king never allowed them to do this despite the many accusations that were being levelled against the Muslims. Are Christians welcomed and looked after in the same way in Islamic nations today?

In a verse revealed to Muhammad, Sura 57:27, Allah states that He has put compassion and mercy in hearts of those who follow Jesus. Therefore, we conclude that if anyone wants to have Allah's mercy and compassion, he or she will find no other way than by following Jesus, the Merciful.

The Word

As we can see from Sura 3:45 (see top of page 101), when the Angel Gabriel appeared to Mary, he informed her of a **Word** from Allah and that **Word** was to be named: Jesus, the Messiah. Mary, having no doubt of her own chastity, could not imagine how such a thing could happen. However, the angel assured her that it was a decree from Allah that must be fulfilled. From the beginning, Jesus was the Word of God and as the Scripture reveals, the Word was with God. God sent the Word into the world through Mary even as it is written in John's Gospel 1:14 "The Word became flesh and dwelt among us (mankind)". It was necessary that the invisible Word should take on flesh, so that people could see him, hear him, and learn from him. This was the living Word, who was made a classic example for mankind.

God spoke to mankind through Jesus Christ. A cassette, when played, repeats exactly what the original speaker spoke and it carries the same weight and authority as if the speaker himself were present. So, as the Word of God, whenever Jesus spoke, it was God Himself who spoke. For Jesus said:

John 14:10 (NIV)
"Don't you believe that I am in the Father, and that the Father is in me? The words I say to you are not just my own. Rather, it is the Father, living in me, who is doing his work."

The Spirit

The Qur'an supports the truth that Jesus had the Spirit of
God in him.

Sura Al Anbiya 21:91
*And (remember) her who guarded her chastity: We breathed
into her of Our Spirit, and We made her and her son a Sign
for all peoples.*

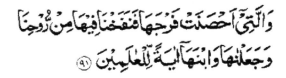

The works of Jesus also testify to this fact. He performed
many deeds which proved his deity, notably he created a
bird (Sura 3:49). In this verse, Jesus describes that as a sign
he makes a bird out of clay and then breathes into so that
the bird becomes alive. Jesus created the bird in the same
manner in which God created Adam. God and Jesus have
the same Spirit and therefore they are able to do the same
work. As the Qur'an has revealed:

Sura Yunus 10:34
*Say "Of your 'partners', can any one originate creation
and repeat it? Say; it is Allah Who originates creation and
repeats it. Then how are ye deluded away (from the truth)?"*

Since Jesus was able to repeat creation, the truth about his nature is made clear.

Muslims describe themselves as a people who have submitted completely to the will of Allah. But without complete submission to the One who is the **Mercy**, the **Word** and the **Spirit** of Allah it is impossible to claim submission to Allah's will.

The Great Commission

Christians are urged to preach the gospel, which means "good news," to everyone. This is a basic duty for every Christian. Jesus said:

John 17:18
"As you have sent me into the world, I have sent them (the disciples) into the world."

This is echoed elsewhere:

Matthew 28:19
"Therefore go and make disciples of all nations, baptising them in the name of the Father and of the Son and of the Holy Spirit, ..."

The Author of the Qur'an also knew of the importance of the gospel and recommended it to the Muslims. They need it for salvation and for spiritual growth. Muslims need Christ. According to the Qur'an, it is the Christians, referred to as "the people of the Book," who are charged with the responsibility of proclaiming the message of the Book, including the Gospel to all people:

Sura Imran 3:187
And remember Allah took a Covenant from the People of
the Book, to make it known and clear to mankind, and not
to hide it; but they threw it away behind their backs, and
purchased with it some miserable gain! And vile was the
bargain they made!

وَإِذْ أَخَذَ اللَّهُ مِيثَاقَ الَّذِينَ أُوتُوا الْكِتَبَ لَتُبَيِّنُنَّهُ

لِلنَّاسِ وَلَا تَكْتُمُونَهُ فَنَبَذُوهُ وَرَاءَ ظُهُورِهِمْ

وَاشْتَرَوْا بِهِ ثَمَنًا قَلِيلًا فَبِئْسَ مَا يَشْتَرُونَ ۞

The great commission is a covenant, and a command, which must be taken with all seriousness. True Christians have often failed in this duty to reach all people with the gospel. However, what God has ordered to be done should not be left undone. Muslims must therefore welcome Christians for peaceful religious discussion. This ordinance is binding. Sura Yunus 10:94 instructs Muslims, including Muhammad himself, to seek clarification from the people of the Book when any doubt arises in the course of reading the Qur'an. Clearly the Qur'an supports the fact, that Muslims need Christ and that they must be prepared to meet Him.

The Second Coming

One may ask, how can Jesus guide the chosen people to God when he is no more with us? The Qur'an provides the answer:

Sura Zukruf 43:61
And (Jesus) shall be a Sign (for the coming of) the Hour (of
Judgement): Therefore have no doubt about the (Hour), but
follow ye Me: This is a Straight Way.

وَإِنَّهُۥ لَعِلْمٌ لِّلسَّاعَةِ فَلَا تَمْتَرُنَّ بِهَا وَاتَّبِعُونِ
هَذَا صِرَاطٌ مُّسْتَقِيمٌ ۝

Jesus is referred to as -*the Sign for the coming of the
hour.* Verses 66 and 69 of Sura 43 warn those sects who
have fallen into disagreement of their fate -*the Penalty of a
Grievous Day!* The Hour would come suddenly upon them
but Allah's servants shall *not fear nor grieve.* This refers to
the Last Hour and establishes the fact that Jesus is coming
again.

Concerning this Second Coming, Christians believe
that at that time Jesus Christ will return for his own people.
In the fields, in the houses, in the shops in the offices,
wherever they are, one person will be taken and another
left behind (Matthew 34:40-42). Only his true believers will
be taken up to be with him in Heaven. All the others will
remain behind for the most frightful of judgements. Only
the wise bridesmaids (according to Matthew 25:1-12), who
are prepared, with spare oil to fill their lamps, as they wait
in the wedding chamber will be allowed to participate. The
foolish ones, in spite of their apparent obedience shall be
left outside without hope.

Some Muslims have quite a different story concerning
Jesus' Second Coming. They say that Jesus Christ did not
complete his mission here and that he will not complete
it until his Second Coming. These Muslims need to know
that, according to the Gospel of John, the last words of Jesus

at the time of his dying on the cross were: "It is finished" (John 19:30). Jesus Christ accomplished his mission and left nothing undone. He finished everything that was to be done (John 17:4).

Abu Hurira, one of the authentic recorders of Mohammed's sayings, reported Muhammad as saying:

By Him, in whose hands my soul is, Jesus Son of Mary will soon descend among you as a JUST JUDGE

(see *The Muslims World League Journal 1982, Vol. 9 Pg. 23*). In these words, the Prophet of Islam himself gave testimony as to the real mission of Jesus Christ at his Second Coming. He is coming as a Just Judge.

Dear Reader, consider yourself: Will you be taken or left? Will you be inside or outside of Jesus' kingdom?

Jesus says:

Luke 13:24-25,27
"Strive to enter in at the strait gate, for many, I say unto you, will seek to enter in and shall not be able. When once the master of the house is risen up and hath shut the door, and ye begin to stand outside and to knock at the door, saying, 'Lord, Lord, open unto us,' and He shall answer and say unto you,…'I tell you, I know you not from whence ye are. Depart from Me, all ye workers of iniquity.' "

Conclusion

Having heard all these appeals from the Bible and from the Qur'an, do you cry out: "What must I do to be saved?" If you do, the answer we have is the same as that of the Apostle Peter:

Acts 2:38-39

"Repent and be baptised, everyone of you, in the name of Jesus Christ for the forgiveness of sins. And you will receive the gift of the Holy Spirit. The promise is for you and your children and for all who are far off - for all whom the Lord our God will call."

And:

Acts 3:19-21

"Repent, then, and turn to God, so that your sins may be wiped out, that times of refreshing may come from the Lord, and that he may send the Christ, who has been appointed for you – even Jesus. He must remain in heaven until the time comes for God to restore everything, as he promised long ago through his holy prophets."

4

WHO IS JESUS?

Jesus In The Qur'an

In the Qur'an, Jesus is identified as *Isa al-Masih*. However, it should be noted that the Arabic name *Isa* does not have the same meaning as the name **Jesus,** which is the Greek version of the Hebrew name **Joshua** or **Jehoshuah** meaning "Jehovah saves." Etymologically, *Isa* seems to be nearer to Esau. The name *Isa* cannot be found in the Arabic translation of the Bible for the name Jesus has been correctly translated into Arabic as **Yasua**. Thus, the Arabic Bible gives a clear testimony of the mission of Jesus Christ as the "Saviour" in the Arabic language.

The Titles of Jesus in the Qur'an

The Qur'an gives Jesus the following names and titles.

1. *Al-Masih* - "the Messiah" (Qur'an 3:45)
   Only Jesus Christ is given this title in the Qur'an with this title. About twenty-five prophets are named in the Qur'an, but only Jesus befits this noble title - *Al-Masih*. *Al-Masih* means "the anointed one" and is the same as Messiah in Hebrew and *Kristos* (Christ) in Greek. Prophets like David (Dawud) and Solomon (Sulaiman) were anointed, yet they never assumed the title *al-Masih*. The oil that was used to anoint them was purchased in Jerusalem, but Jesus was anointed from above.

2. *Kalimatuhu* - "His Word" (Qur'an 4:171)
   By implication the Qur'an refers to Jesus as God's Word, the Word of God, or *Kalimatu'llah*.
   This particular title has become a point of strong controversy among the Muslim community, with regards to the correct meaning of *Kalimat*. The translators of the Qur'an into English differ in opinion as to whether to translate *Kalimat* as "word" with a small "w" or "Word" with a capital "W." The whole world is yet to receive a *fatwa* (a religious or judicial decision) on that.
   It is recognised that each of the translations, "word" or "Word" connotes a different meaning. Whereas the Bible unashamedly refers to Jesus as "the Word" (John 1:1f), Muslims reject the teaching in this passage. Therefore, the Qur'anic translators have tended to downplay the role of Jesus as simply "a word."

3. *Ruhu-minhu* - "a Spirit from Him" (Qur'an 4:171; 21:91)
   By implication, Jesus is referred to as a Spirit from God
   (*Ruhu-mina -llah*). God speaks of Jesus as of "Our
   Spirit". Is this Spirit divine? Let the Muslims answer
   this question sincerely.

   In comparison with other prophets, we observe that
   Allah sees:

Adam	as *Safiyu'llah*	- the chosen of Allah;
Noah	as *Nabiyu'llah*	- the preacher of Allah;
Abraham	as *Khalilu'llah*	- the friend of Allah;
Moses	as *Kalimu'llah*	- the converser with Allah;
Muhammad	as *Rasulu'llah*	- the Messenger of Allah;

   But only

Jesus	as *Ruhu'llah*	- the Spirit of Allah.

   In Islam, Allah cannot be likened to anyone, Qur'an
   112:4. He is far above the prophets, as is clearly shown
   in respect of their titles. There is a clear separation
   from the being of Allah when these titles are carefully
   analysed. However, when it comes to Jesus, that
   separation is eliminated, and as "His Spirit," he is
   brought very close to the very being of Allah.

   Do we not recognise that by identifying Jesus so closely
   with Himself, Allah is revealing the deity of Jesus
   Christ, which Muslims vehemently object to? Muslims
   have rather reduced Jesus to the same level as the other
   prophets, with the exception of Muhammad who they
   consider as the greatest of all.

4. *Wajihan Fi'dunya wa'lakhirah* – "Illustrious in the world and the Hereafter" (Qur'an 3:45, Pickthall). This title is what the Qur'an has disclosed to us about Jesus Christ. However, this is no new revelation to the Christian because the same truth is contained in the Bible. Indeed, Christians knew this truth about Jesus long before the birth of Muhammad.

Waraqa Ibn Naufal, the man whom Muhammad consulted after he (Muhammad) began to receive supernatural messages, was a Christian monk. He surely knew and read from the Bible that Jesus is seated at the right hand of God:

Ephesians 1:20-21 (NIV)
...He (God) raised him (Jesus) from the dead and seated him at His right hand in the heavenly realms far above all heavenly rulers and authorities, powers and dominions and every name or title that can be given, not only in the present age but also in the one which is to come.

Taking the contents of the Qur'an alone, none of the prophets mentioned in it can be compared to Jesus as far as His heavenly position is concerned.

Jesus clearly revealed his heavenly origin in the Gospel:

John 6:14
"What if you see the Son of Man ascend to where He was before?"

John 8:23, 58
"You are from below; I am from above. You are of this world; I am not of this world." ..."I tell you the truth," Jesus answered, "before Abraham was, I am!"

If we consider the opinion of a Muslim scholar, we see that when Hammudah Abdalaati wrote his book "Islam in Focus," he dismissed the various opinions of Muslims concerning the crucifixion, death and ascension of Jesus as having little bearing on Islamic belief. To him, what is important and binding on the Muslim is what Allah has revealed. Thus, as far as he is concerned, the complexity on this issue can be solved by the revelation given to Muhammad that Jesus was not crucified (Qur'an 4:157) but:

Qur'an 4:158
Nay, Allah raised him up unto Himself; and Allah is Exalted in Power, Wise;

بَل رَّفَعَهُ اللَّهُ إِلَيْهِ وَكَانَ اللَّهُ عَزِيزًا حَكِيمًا ۝

On the other hand, Hammudah Abdalaati, surprisingly, for one who only takes what the Qur'an says, treats the virgin birth of Jesus very lightly, comparing it to mythological figures like Bacchus, Apollo, Adonis and Horus who were said to be virgin-born gods. However, we might ask, where in the Qur'an is it revealed that these gods were born through virgin birth? In contrast, the accounts of the angelic announcement of Jesus' birth to Mary in Qur'an clearly show that Mary was chaste and that God Himself would intervene to enable her to conceive as a virgin (Qur'an 3:45-47; 19:16-22).

In fact, this same account was recorded by Luke centuries before the birth of Muhammad. However, Muslims have dismissed Luke's account as hearsay on the grounds that Luke was not one of the apostles appointed by Jesus Christ. Nonetheless, since the acclaimed hearsay has turned out to be a revelation from Allah to Muhammad, it behoves us to take it with the same level of seriousness.

Without a doubt, the Qur'an bears testimony to the virgin birth of Jesus Christ in contrast to that of Muhammad (Qur'an 21:91).

On the other hand, the Qur'an completely rejects the Christian doctrine of the Trinity, but at the same time misrepresents it as "the Father, the Son and the Mother," contrary to "the Father, the Son and the Holy Spirit" given by Jesus in Matthew 28:19.

Qur'an 5:119
And behold Allah will say: "O Jesus, the son of Mary! Did thou say unto men, 'worship me (Jesus, the Son) and my mother (Mary, the Mother) as gods in derogation of Allah (God -the Father)'? He will say: "Glory to Thee! Never could I say what I had no right (to say). Had I said such a thing, Thou wouldst indeed have known it. Thou knowest what is in my heart, though I know not what is in Thine. For Thou knowest in full all that is hidden."

وَإِذْ قَالَ اللّٰهُ يَعِيسَى ابْنَ مَرْيَمَ ءَأَنتَ قُلْتَ لِلنَّاسِ اتَّخِذُونِى وَأُمِّىَ إِلَهَيْنِ مِن دُونِ اللّٰهِ قَالَ سُبْحَانَكَ مَا يَكُونُ لِى أَنْ أَقُولَ مَا لَيْسَ لِى بِحَقٍّ إِن كُنتُ قُلْتُهُ فَقَدْ عَلِمْتَهُ تَعْلَمُ مَا فِى نَفْسِى وَلَا أَعْلَمُ مَا فِى نَفْسِكَ إِنَّكَ أَنتَ عَلَّامُ الْغُيُوبِ ۝

Muslims are quick to point out that the word "Trinity" cannot be found in the Bible and yet, it seems that they have forgotten that likewise the word "*Tawheed*" (the "oneness" of God), which is the first article of the Islamic faith, cannot be found in the Qur'an. However, just as both the Bible and the Qur'an make statements that attest to *Tawheed*, so the Bible also makes clear statements that attest to the truth that God, although being one, reveals himself in three persons (the Trinity). This truth is reasonable and acceptable to everyone who sees Jesus as above all other human beings.

It will be difficult for Muslims to appreciate this mystery about God, since it appears that Muhammad did not get clear teaching from those, such as Waraqa Ibn Nauful, whom he consulted about Christianity.

The Miracles of Jesus

The Qur'an reveals that Jesus was able to perform miracles:

Qur'an 3:49, (cf 5:113)
And (appoint him) an apostle to the Children of Israel, (with this message). "I have come to you, with a Sign from your Lord, in that I make for you out of clay, as it were, the figure of a bird, and breathe into it, and it becomes a bird by Allah's leave: And I heal those born blind, and the lepers, and I quicken the dead, by Allah's leave; and I declare to you what ye eat, and what ye store in your houses. Surely therein is a Sign for you if ye did believe;"

وَرَسُولًا إِلَىٰ بَنِىٓ إِسۡرَٰٓءِيلَ أَنِّى قَدۡ جِئۡتُكُم بِـَٔايَةٍ

مِّن رَّبِّكُمۡ أَنِّىٓ أَخۡلُقُ لَكُم مِّنَ ٱلطِّينِ كَهَيۡـَٔةِ ٱلطَّيۡرِ

فَأَنفُخُ فِيهِ فَيَكُونُ طَيۡرَۢا بِإِذۡنِ ٱللَّهِۖ وَأُبۡرِئُ ٱلۡأَكۡمَهَ

وَٱلۡأَبۡرَصَ وَأُحۡىِ ٱلۡمَوۡتَىٰ بِإِذۡنِ ٱللَّهِۖ وَأُنَبِّئُكُم

بِمَا تَأۡكُلُونَ وَمَا تَدَّخِرُونَ فِى بُيُوتِكُمۡۚ إِنَّ فِى

ذَٰلِكَ لَأٓيَةٗ لَّكُمۡ إِن كُنتُم مُّؤۡمِنِينَ ٤٩

- Miracle No.1: Jesus Christ created a living bird out of clay
- Miracle No.2: Jesus Christ healed those born blind
- Miracle No.3: Jesus Christ healed lepers
- Miracle No.4: Jesus Christ brought the dead back to life

While the miracle of creating the living bird out of clay cannot be traced in the Holy Bible, details of the healing of the blind and lepers and the raising of the dead can be found, (for example: Matthew 11:5; John 9:1-7; Mark 1:40-42; Luke 7:12-15). In addition, Qur'an 3:49 reveals that Jesus had supernatural knowledge as the Bible also shows (John 1:47-48).

That Jesus created a bird, as the Qur'an has revealed, must be considered a great miracle. However, Muslims are divided as to whether it should be taken as true or metaphorical or whether it is false. The line of argument of the Ahmadis is enlightening in this respect. They argue that it is metaphorical on the basis that there is no mention of the miracle in the Bible. For, if Jesus had really created birds, there is no reason why the Bible should have failed to mention it, especially since the creating of birds was a miracle the like of which had never been shown before by any messenger of God. Indeed, the mention of such a miracle would certainly have established his great superiority over all the other prophets and would have lent some support to the claim of divinity, which they argue has been foisted on him by his later followers.

From their argument we can therefore establish the following points:

a. There is no mention of the miracle in the Bible.
b. There is no reason for its omission.
c. The creating of birds is unique and superior.

d. No other prophet of God ever had the ability to create anything.
e. The miracle establishes the superiority of Jesus over all other known prophets.

We will study the full implications of these observations in the following section.

Is Jesus God?

As we have seen in the previous sections, the titles and miracles of Jesus that are revealed in the Qur'an support the Biblical claim that Jesus is God (Romans 9:5, 1 John 5:20). In case the reader is in doubt, we will continue by examining the evidence for this claim in more detail.

Only God Can Create

Qur'an 10:34

Say: "Of your 'partners', can any originate creation and repeat it?" Say: "It is Allah Who originates creation and repeats it: Then how are ye deluded away (from the truth)?"

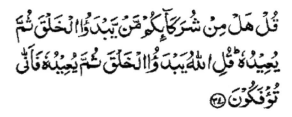

The above verse from Qur'an indicates that the false gods cannot create. The ability to create is attributed to Allah alone. In the Qur'an, the act of creation -*khalq* has not been attributed to any other being or thing apart from Allah.

Qur'an 13:16
Say: "Who is the Lord and Sustainer of the heavens and the earth?" say: "(It is) Allah." say: "Do ye then take (for worship) protectors other than Him, such as have no power either for good or for harm to themselves?" Say: "Are the blind equal with those who see? Or the depths of darkness equal with Light?" Or do they assign to Allah partners who have created (anything) as He has created, so that the creation seemed to them similar? Say: "Allah is the Creator of all things: He is the One, the Supreme and Irresistible."

قُلْ مَنْ رَّبُّ السَّمَوَاتِ وَالْأَرْضِ قُلِ اللهُ قُلْ
أَفَاتَّخَذْتُمْ مِّنْ دُونِهِ أَوْلِيَاءَ لَا يَمْلِكُونَ لِأَنْفُسِهِمْ
نَفْعًا وَّلَا ضَرًّا قُلْ هَلْ يَسْتَوِي الْأَعْمَى وَالْبَصِيرُ
أَمْ هَلْ تَسْتَوِي الظُّلُمَاتُ وَالنُّورُ أَمْ جَعَلُوا لِلّهِ
شُرَكَاءَ خَلَقُوا كَخَلْقِهِ فَتَشَابَهَ الْخَلْقُ عَلَيْهِمْ
قُلِ اللهُ خَالِقُ كُلِّ شَيْءٍ وَهُوَ الْوَاحِدُ الْقَهَّارُ ﴿١٦﴾

Qur'an 31:11
Such is the Creation of Allah: Now show Me what is there that others besides Him have created?

هَذَا خَلْقُ اللهِ فَأَرُونِي مَاذَا خَلَقَ الَّذِينَ مِنْ دُونِهِ
بَلِ الظَّالِمُونَ فِي ضَلَالٍ مُبِينٍ ﴿١١﴾

Muslims have found it difficult and impossible to accept the deity of Jesus Christ as the Bible reveals. This is because, such superiority stands contrary to the Qur'an as it does not specifically declare the deity of Christ. Rather, the Qur'an condemns the associating of partners or likening other beings or things to God as "Shirk" which is regarded as the greatest sin of Islam.

Notwithstanding, when we examine the Qur'an critically and with an open mind, we can see that it does reveal the deity of Jesus. However, it is true to say that this truth is at the same time watered down.

Let us make a further study of the miracle revealed in the Qur'an (3:49; 5:113 – see top of page 117) in which Jesus created birds.

This a miracle the like of which had never been shown before by any other prophet of Allah. Instead of pondering over this miracle, many have explained it away by saying it was Allah who gave Jesus the help to do it. However, the question remains, why was it given to Jesus and no other prophet?

We will come to understand this unique miracle better by reminding ourselves that the greatest sin in Islam is "Shirk." For the Qur'an (*Qur'an 112:4*) emphasises that ...*there is none like unto Him.* Yet we need to remind ourselves that the same Qur'an describes Jesus as a Spirit from Allah (*Ruh-mina-llah*) and Allah speaks of Jesus as being "*of Our Spirit*" (see pages 113).

We cannot avoid the question: Is this Spirit divine? Please be bold to answer! As we have already seen, of all the prophets, Allah sees only Jesus Christ as *Ruhu'llah* - "the Spirit of Allah." Can you not see the superiority of Jesus? Since Jesus is the "Spirit of Allah" we should not be surprised or feel uncomfortable if he repeats creation. As the Qur'an emphasises, it is the false gods that are incapable of such a feat.

Qur'an 22:73
O men! Here is a parable set forth! Listen to it! Those on whom, besides Allah, ye call, cannot create (even) a fly, if they all met together for the purpose! And if the fly should snatch away anything from them, they would have no power to release it from the fly. Feeble are those who petition and those whom they petition!

يَٰٓأَيُّهَا ٱلنَّاسُ ضُرِبَ مَثَلٌ فَٱسْتَمِعُوا۟ لَهُۥٓ إِنَّ ٱلَّذِينَ تَدْعُونَ مِن دُونِ ٱللَّهِ لَن يَخْلُقُوا۟ ذُبَابًا وَلَوِ ٱجْتَمَعُوا۟ لَهُۥ وَإِن يَسْلُبْهُمُ ٱلذُّبَابُ شَيْـًٔا لَّا يَسْتَنقِذُوهُ مِنْهُ ضَعُفَ ٱلطَّالِبُ وَٱلْمَطْلُوبُ ۝

As we have already seen, the Ahmadis have raised the question: "If Jesus had really created birds why is there no mention of it in the Bible?" On this ground they dismiss the miracle as figurative. Surprisingly, these same people endorse the fact that such a miracle would certainly establish the superiority of Jesus over all the other prophets. Praise God!

We need to be clear in our minds and humbly accept the truth that Jesus did create birds, an act that can only be done by God (Allah). This indisputably establishes the deity of Jesus Christ. The fact that this miracle of Jesus was not mentioned in the Bible cannot cancel his deity. After all, the Apostle John tells us:

John 21:25
And there are also many other things which Jesus did, which, if they should be written every one, I suppose that even the world itself could not contain the books that should be written.

John 20:30-31
And many other signs truly did Jesus in the presence of His disciples, which are not written in this book. But these are written, that ye might believe that Jesus is the Christ, the Son of God, and that believing, ye might have life through His name.

Indeed, for those who are willing to see, the Bible reveals that, not only did Jesus create birds, but he was responsible for the whole of creation!

Colossians 1:16
For by Him were all things created that are in heaven and that are on earth, visible and invisible, whether they be thrones or dominions or principalities or powers: all things were created by Him and for Him.

John 1:1-3
In the beginning was the Word, and the Word was with God, and the Word was God. The same was in the beginning with God. All things were made by Him, and without Him was not anything made that was made.

If we require further evidence of the deity of Jesus, we must acknowledge that even death could not hold him as it held others. Furthermore, the Qur'an declares that Jesus is holy:

Qur'an 19:19

He said: "Nay, I am only a messenger from thy Lord, (to announce) to thee the gift of a holy son."

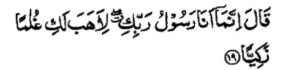

Who, apart from God is holy?

Finally, we know that Satan can remind all the prophets of their sin, that is with the exception of Jesus, *Ruhu'llah –* The Spirit of God, for the Spirit of God cannot and does not sin.

In conclusion, Jesus, the Holy One who does not sin, who is the Spirit of God and who creates birds, an act attributed only to God, must be God. Do you still doubt his divinity?

Jesus – The only one qualified to be Saviour

The great story of salvation and the need for guidance can be traced back through the Bible and the Qur'an to the creation of humanity. Indeed, we may argue that the story of humanity and the story of salvation are one and the same. Let us then follow this story as narrated by the Bible and the Qur'an.

1. **God created Mankind**
    God created man and gave him life, wisdom, knowledge and dominion.

Genesis 2:7
"And the LORD GOD formed man of the dust of the ground, and breathed into his nostrils the breath of life; and man became a living soul."

Qur'an 32:7, 9
He Who has made everything which He has created Most Good: He began the creation of man with (nothing more than) clay,...

But He fashioned him in due proportion, and breathed into him something of His spirit. And He gave you (the faculties of) hearing and sight and feeling (and understanding): Little thanks do ye give!

الَّذِىٓ أَحْسَنَ كُلَّ شَىْءٍ خَلَقَهُ وَبَدَأَ خَلْقَ ٱلْإِنسَانِ مِن طِينٍ ۞

ثُمَّ سَوَّىٰهُ وَنَفَخَ فِيهِ مِن رُّوحِهِ وَجَعَلَ لَكُمُ ٱلسَّمْعَ وَٱلْأَبْصَٰرَ وَٱلْأَفْـِٔدَةَ قَلِيلًا مَّا تَشْكُرُونَ ۞

2. God provided for Mankind's Needs

God placed man in a garden of plenty and provided all that he needed. All that God gave him was good.

Genesis 2:16-17
"And the LORD God commanded the man, saying, of every tree of the garden thou mayest freely eat: But of the tree of the knowledge of good and evil, thou shalt not eat of it: for in the day that thou eatest thereof thou shalt surely die."

Qur'an 2:35 (cf 7:19)
"We said: "O Adam! Dwell thou and thy wife in the Garden; and eat of the bountiful things therein as (where and when) ye will; but approach not this tree, or ye run into harm and transgression."

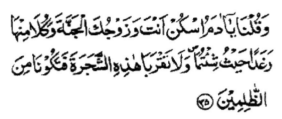

3. God demanded Obedience
God revealed His will to man so that man was not left in ignorance. (see Genesis 2:17 and Qur'an 2:35 above).

4. Satan vowed to take Revenge

Qur'an 7:16-17

He said: "Because thus hast thrown me out of the way, lo! I will lie in wait for them on thy straight way: Then will I assault them from before them and behind them, from their right and their left: Nor wilt thou find, in most of them, gratitude (for they mercies)."

5. Satan enters the Garden
Satan tried his tricks on mankind and succeeded in deceiving them.

Genesis 3:1-10
"Now the serpent was more subtle than any beast of the field which the LORD God had made. And he said

unto the woman, Yea, hath God said, ye shall not eat of every tree of the garden? And the woman said unto the serpent, we may eat of the fruit of the trees of the garden: But of the fruit of the tree which is in the midst of the garden, God hath said, ye shall not eat of it, neither shall you touch it, lest ye die. And the serpent said unto the woman, ye shall not surely die: For God doth know that in the day ye eat thereof, then your eyes shall be opened, and ye shall be as gods, knowing good and evil. And when the woman saw that the tree was good for food, and that it was pleasant to the eyes, and a tree to be desired to make one wise, she took of the fruit thereof, and did eat, and gave also unto her husband with her; and he did eat. And the eyes of them both were opened, and they knew that they were naked; and they sewed fig leaves together, and made themselves aprons. And they heard the voice of the LORD God walking in the garden in the cool of the day: and Adam and his wife hid themselves from the presence of the LORD God amongst the trees of the garden. And the LORD God called unto Adam, and said unto him, where art thou? And he said, I heard thy voice in the garden, and I was afraid, because I was naked; and I hid myself."

Qur'an 7:20-22 (cf 2:36)

Then began Satan to whisper suggestions to them, bringing openly before their minds all their shame that was hidden from them (before): he said: "Your Lord only forbade you this tree, lest ye should come angels or such beings as live for ever." And he swore to them both, that he was their sincere adviser. So by deceit he brought about them all: when they tasted of the tree, their shame became manifest to them, and they began to sew together the leaves of the garden over their bodies. And their Lord called unto them: "Did I not forbid you that tree, and tell you that Satan was an avowed enemy unto you?"

فَوَسْوَسَ لَهُمَا الشَّيْطَٰنُ لِيُبْدِىَ لَهُمَا مَا وُۥرِىَ عَنْهُمَا مِن سَوْءَٰتِهِمَا وَقَالَ مَا نَهَىٰكُمَا رَبُّكُمَا عَنْ هَٰذِهِ الشَّجَرَةِ إِلَّا أَن تَكُونَا مَلَكَيْنِ أَوْ تَكُونَا مِنَ الْخَٰلِدِينَ ۝ وَقَاسَمَهُمَا إِنِّى لَكُمَا لَمِنَ النَّٰصِحِينَ ۝ فَدَلَّىٰهُمَا بِغُرُورٍ فَلَمَّا ذَاقَا الشَّجَرَةَ بَدَتْ لَهُمَا سَوْءَٰتُهُمَا وَطَفِقَا يَخْصِفَٰنِ عَلَيْهِمَا مِن وَرَقِ الْجَنَّةِ وَنَادَىٰهُمَا رَبُّهُمَا أَلَمْ أَنْهَكُمَا عَن تِلْكُمَا الشَّجَرَةِ وَأَقُل لَّكُمَا إِنَّ الشَّيْطَٰنَ لَكُمَا عَدُوٌّ مُّبِينٌ ۝

6. Mankind disobeyed God

Adam and Eve took Satan's counsel and listened to him rather than to God. Disobedience to God is sin and so they sinned by choosing to go their own way.

Genesis 3:6

And when the woman saw that the tree was good for food, and that it was pleasant to the eyes, and a tree to be desired to make one wise, she took of the fruit thereof, and did eat, and gave also unto her husband with her; and he did eat.

Genesis 3:11
And he said, "who told thee that thou wast naked;
Hast thou eaten of the tree, whereof I commanded thee
that thou shouldest not eat?"

7. **Mankind was separated from God**
God hates sin and therefore sin separates people from
God.

Genesis 3:23
Therefore the LORD God sent him forth from the Garden
of Eden, to till the ground from whence he was taken.

Qur'an 7:24
*(God) said: "Get ye down, with enmity between yourselves.
On earth will be your dwelling-place and your means of
livelihood, for a time."*

قَالَ اهْبِطُوا بَعْضُكُمْ لِبَعْضٍ عَدُوٌّ وَلَكُمْ فِى
الْأَرْضِ مُسْتَقَرٌّ وَمَتَاعٌ إِلَى حِينٍ ۝
قَالَ فِيهَا تَحْيَوْنَ وَفِيهَا تَمُوتُونَ وَمِنْهَا
تُخْرَجُونَ ۝

Isaiah 59:1-2
"Behold, the Lord's hand is not shortened, that it
cannot save; neither his ear heavy, that it cannot hear:
But your iniquities have separated between you and
your God, and your sins have hid his face from you,
that he will not hear."

Qur'an 2:38
"We said: "Get ye down all from here; and if, as is sure,
there comes to you guidance from Me, whosoever follows my
guidance, on them shall be no fear, nor shall they grieve."

8. The Wages Of Sin

To be away from God's presence is to be spiritually dead and physical death also entered the world because of sin. The whole family of Adam became affected and all have sinned bringing the same judgement upon themselves.

Romans 3:23 (NIV)
For all have sinned and fall short of the glory of God,

Romans 6:23 (NIV)
For the wages of sin is death; but the gift of God is eternal life in Christ Jesus our Lord.

Qur'an 16:61 (cf 35:45)
"If God were to punish men for their wrong-doing, he would not leave, on the (earth), a single living creature: But He gives them respite for a stated term: when their term expires, they would not be able to delay (the punishment) for a single hour, just as they would not be able to anticipate it (for a single hour)."

وَلَوْ يُؤَاخِذُ اللّٰهُ النَّاسَ بِظُلْمِهِم مَّا تَرَكَ عَلَيْهَا
مِن دَآبَّةٍ وَلَٰكِن يُؤَخِّرُهُمْ إِلَىٰٓ أَجَلٍ مُّسَمًّى فَإِذَا
جَآءَ أَجَلُهُمْ لَا يَسْتَأْخِرُونَ سَاعَةً وَلَا يَسْتَقْدِمُونَ ۝

Hadith:

Anaaso Kuluhum, banuu Adama Wa Aadamo min turaabin.

The first Adam fell and through his disobedience, he failed to maintain his Islam (submission to God). Adam was supposed to be an example of submission to guide us to God.

9. God sent the Prophets

They were supposed to live above sin, maintaining pure Islam so that they could guide people to God.

Qur'an 7:35

"O ye children of Adam! Whenever there come to you Apostles from amongst you, rehearsing my signs unto you, those who are righteous and mend (their lives), on them shall be no fear nor shall they grieve."

يَٰبَنِىٓ ءَادَمَ إِمَّا يَأْتِيَنَّكُمْ رُسُلٌ مِّنكُمْ يَقُصُّونَ عَلَيْكُمْ ءَايَٰتِى فَمَنِ ٱتَّقَىٰ وَأَصْلَحَ فَلَا خَوْفٌ عَلَيْهِمْ وَلَا هُمْ يَحْزَنُونَ ۝

All the prophets are descendants of Adam and all of them fell into sin:

Adam fell in sin	Qur'an	7	:23
Noah fell in sin	Qur'an	11	:47
Moses fell in sin	Qur'an	28	:16
David fell in sin	Qur'an	38	:24
Solomon fell in sin	Qur'an	38	:35
Muhammad fell in sin	Qur'an	48	:2

10. God sent Guidance to save Mankind

Qur'an 2:38
*"We said: "Get ye down all from here; and if, as is sure,
there comes to you guidance from Me, whosoever follows my
guidance, on them shall be no fear, nor shall they grieve."*

قُلْنَا اهْبِطُوا مِنْهَا جَمِيعًا فَإِمَّا يَأْتِيَنَّكُم مِّنِّي هُدًى
فَمَن تَبِعَ هُدَايَ فَلَا خَوْفٌ عَلَيْهِمْ وَلَا هُمْ يَحْزَنُونَ ۝
وَالَّذِينَ كَفَرُوا وَكَذَّبُوا بِآيَاتِنَا أُولَٰئِكَ أَصْحَابُ النَّارِ
هُمْ فِيهَا خَالِدُونَ ۝

This guidance should be different, it must not fail like
the previous prophets. This time God sent His Word.

Qur'an 3:39
*"While he was standing in prayer in the chamber, the angels
called unto him: "God doth give thee glad tidings of Yahya,
witnessing the truth of a Word from God, and (be besides)
noble, chaste, and a Prophet, of the (goodly) company of the
righteous."*

فَنَادَتْهُ الْمَلَائِكَةُ وَهُوَ قَائِمٌ يُصَلِّي فِي الْمِحْرَابِ
أَنَّ اللَّهَ يُبَشِّرُكَ بِيَحْيَىٰ مُصَدِّقًا بِكَلِمَةٍ مِّنَ اللَّهِ
وَسَيِّدًا وَحَصُورًا وَنَبِيًّا مِّنَ الصَّالِحِينَ ۝

This Word was Jesus Christ.

Qur'an 3:45
"Behold! The angels said: "O Mary! God giveth thee glad
tidings of a Word from Him: his name will be Christ Jesus,
the son of Mary, held in honour in this world and the
hereafter and of (the company of) those nearest to God;"

إِذْ قَالَتِ الْمَلَائِكَةُ يَامَرْيَمُ إِنَّ اللَّهَ يُبَشِّرُكِ بِكَلِمَةٍ
مِّنْهُ اسْمُهُ الْمَسِيحُ عِيسَى ابْنُ مَرْيَمَ وَجِيهًا
فِي الدُّنْيَا وَالْآخِرَةِ وَمِنَ الْمُقَرَّبِينَ ۝
وَيُكَلِّمُ النَّاسَ فِي الْمَهْدِ وَكَهْلًا وَمِنَ
الصَّالِحِينَ ۝

11. The Word came to deal with Sin

John 1:29 (NIV)
The next day, John saw Jesus coming towards him and
said, "Look, the Lamb of God, who takes away the sin
of the world!"

Satan was not able to deceive Jesus or cause him to sin.

Matthew 4:4-11 (NIV)
"Jesus answered, "It is written: 'Man does not live on
bread alone, but on every word that comes from the
mouth of God.' Then the devil took him to the holy
city and had him stand on the highest point of the
temple. "If you are the Son of God," he said, "throw
yourself down. For it is written: 'He will command his
angles concerning you, and they will lift you up in their

hands, so that you will not strike your foot against a stone." Jesus answered him, "It is also written: 'Do not put the Lord your God to the test." Again, the devil took him to a very high mountain and showed him all the kingdoms of the world and their splendour. "All this I will give you," he said, "if you will bow down and worship me." Jesus said to him, "Away from me, Satan! For it is written: 'Worship the Lord you God, and serve him only.' Then the devil left him, and angels came and attended him."

Jesus remained holy and sinless.

Qur'an 19:19
"He said: "Nay, I am only a messenger from thy Lord, (To announce) to thee the gift of a holy son."

Hebrews 4:15 (NIV)
...one who has been tempted in every way, just as we are tempted – yet without sin.

Since Jesus has no burden of sin to bare, he is qualified to help others.

Qur'an 35:18
"Nor can a bearer of burdens bear another's burden. If one heavily laden should call another to (bear) his load, not the least portion of it can be carried (by the other), even though he be nearly related. Thou canst but admonish such as fear their Lord unseen and establish regular prayer. And whoever purifies himself does so for the benefit of his own soul; and the destination (of all) is to God."

وَلَا تَزِرُ وَازِرَةٌ وِزْرَ أُخْرَىٰ وَإِن تَدْعُ مُثْقَلَةٌ
إِلَىٰ حِمْلِهَا لَا يُحْمَلْ مِنْهُ شَىْءٌ وَلَوْ كَانَ ذَا قُرْبَىٰ
إِنَّمَا تُنذِرُ الَّذِينَ يَخْشَوْنَ رَبَّهُم بِالْغَيْبِ وَ
أَقَامُوا الصَّلَوٰةَ وَمَن تَزَكَّىٰ فَإِنَّمَا يَتَزَكَّىٰ لِنَفْسِهِ
وَإِلَى اللَّهِ الْمَصِيرُ ۝

He therefore, calls those who are burdened to come to him.

Matthew 11:28 (NIV)
"Come to me, all you who are weary and burdened, and I will give you rest."

He is the way to God.

John 14:6 (NIV)
Jesus answered, "I am the way, the truth and the life. No one comes to the Father except through me.

He is the gate through which the sheep can enter the fold.

John. 10:7 (NIV)
Therefore Jesus said again, "I tell you the truth, I am the gate for the sheep."

He is the only one qualified to be our Saviour and therefore, he is the only person qualified to judge. The world awaits him for judgement.

Qur'an 43:61
"And (Jesus) shall be a sign (for the coming of) the hour (of judgement): Therefore have no doubt about the (Hour, but follow ye me: this is a straight way."

وَإِنَّهُ لَعِلْمٌ لِّلسَّاعَةِ فَلَا تَمْتَرُنَّ بِهَا وَاتَّبِعُونِ هَٰذَا صِرَاطٌ مُّسْتَقِيمٌ ۝

5

THE COMFORTER –
THE HOLY SPIRIT OR MUHAMMAD?

The Great Controversy

According to the Qur'an, Jesus said,

> *Sura 61:6*
> *"O Children of Israel! I am the apostle of Allah (sent) to you, confirming the Law (which came) before me, and giving Glad Tidings of an Apostle to come after me, whose name shall be Ahmad."*

وَإِذۡ قَالَ عِيسَى ٱبۡنُ مَرۡيَمَ يَـٰبَنِىٓ إِسۡرَآءِيلَ إِنِّى
رَسُولُ ٱللَّهِ إِلَيۡكُم مُّصَدِّقٗا لِّمَا بَيۡنَ يَدَىَّ مِنَ
ٱلتَّوۡرَىٰةِ وَمُبَشِّرَۢا بِرَسُولٖ يَأۡتِى مِنۢ بَعۡدِى
ٱسۡمُهُۥٓ أَحۡمَدُ

Ahmad is essentially the same name as Muhammad and both names mean "The Praised One." However, there is no record in the Bible of such a saying by Jesus nor is the name Ahmad mentioned anywhere. This is disturbing for Muslims since they accept that the Gospel contains the sayings and actions of Jesus.

However, in the Gospel of John, when Jesus was preparing his disciples for his departure he did speak about a "**Comforter**" who was to come after him (John 14:16, 26; 15:26 and 16:7). This word "Comforter" in the English of the King James Version of the Bible is used to translate the Greek word *Paraklētos.* It can also be translated as "Advocate" or "Counsellor" (New International Version).

The Muslim Doctors contend that *Paraklētos* is a corruption of another Greek word – *Periklytos*, which they argue means "Praised One" and would be the translation of "Ahmad" in the Greek. They therefore insist that *Periklytos* was the original word occurring in the Greek manuscript of John's Gospel and that Christians altered this word to conceal the evidence for the coming of the Prophet Muhammad.

Those who contend that there has been a falsification of the name, do not however, have any problem with the nature and functions of the **Comforter** as given by Jesus in the Gospels. They maintain that in every way Muhammad fulfilled these functions and may therefore be identified as the one described as "Comforter" in the Bible.

On the other hand, Christians have understood clearly from Jesus' words and the context that the Comforter is the Holy Spirit, the third member of the Godhead.

For the sake of our investigation into the real identity of the "Comforter," therefore, it becomes imperative that we study every truth about the Comforter as based on the descriptive roles given by Jesus, rather than focusing on the name itself.

We will use the Qur'an and the Bible as the only authoritative and reliable sources of reference, for information about Muhammad and the Comforter. From these we will determine whether the nature and works of the Comforter befits Muhammad.

Readers are entreated to see the Qur'an in the same way that Muslims view it, as a Holy Book, containing the exact words of Allah. Whatever is said about Muhammad in the Qur'an must therefore be taken as the absolute truth. To have any doubt about it amounts to a denial of faith in Allah's word.

Another Comforter

We now begin a systematic search through the Qur'an and the Bible for absolute truths about the **Comforter** which Jesus spoke of in the Bible. Let us pray against any spiritual blindness in the name of God.

Dear Reader, join me and turn your Bible to the fourteenth chapter of the Gospel of John and read the sixteenth verse:

John 14:16
"I will pray the Father, and He shall give you **another comforter**, that **He** may abide with you forever".

The above statement of Jesus presupposes that there has been an earlier Comforter, that is the First Advocate. The First Advocate was Christ Jesus, according to the First Book of John, chapter 2 verse 1. This same Jesus was the Word of God (Qur'an 3:45, John 1:1), who became flesh (John 1:14) and dwelt among us to comfort us. Having established the identity of the first Comforter, we shall continue our search for the second Advocate who is described as "**Another Comforter.**"

The Eternal Nature

The Muslim doctors contend that since the Comforter is referred to with the pronoun "He," he must be a human being. However, note how Jesus ended his statement about the **Comforter** by declaring to us that, "He will **abide with you forever.**" Now, without the slightest doubt, Muhammad could not abide with us forever, and his tomb can be reliably located at Medina near Mecca in Saudi Arabia, having died in AD 632.

In answer to this, the Muslim scholars have argued that it is the words of Muhammad that still abide with us as contained in the Qur'an. However it must be clearly noted that, Jesus did **not** say the **words** of the Comforter would abide with us forever, but that the Comforter **himself** would abide with us forever. Furthermore, the words of Qur'an are not Muhammad's words but those of Allah. Muhammad's words would rather be found in the Hadith (the sayings of Muhammad).

May God grant us Patience and Show us the Straight Path. Amen!

The Spiritual Nature

Jesus throws more light on the nature of the said **Comforter** by identifying him as the Spirit (*Ruh*). In John 14 :16-17 and John 15: 26, Jesus called the Comforter the "**Spirit of Truth**" (*Ruh-ul-Haqq*) and in John 14:26 the "**Holy Spirit**" (*Ruh-ul-Quddus*).

The Muslim Scholars however, still maintain that Jesus was speaking about a human being and that since the word *pneuma*, "spirit," in Greek is neuter, Jesus would have used the pronoun "it" if he was referring to a spirit.

In contrast Christians argue that **"He"** indicates a personal being but not necessarily a human being. After all, when we speak of God we also use the pronoun **"He"** and yet the Bible tells us that "God is Spirit." He is a distinct person but not a human being. In any case, the Muslim scholars are not being consistent because in the Qur'an (Sura 4:171), Jesus is described as a "Spirit proceeding from Him (God)" and yet they do not deny that Jesus was a human being. Indeed in their efforts to persuade us that Muhammad is the Comforter, they state that Muhammad is the Spirit of Truth and yet Spirit here is also in the neuter gender as we explain below.

In stating that the word "spirit" is neuter in the Greek language, the Muslims scholars are correct. However, they have failed to recognise certain facts.

Firstly, the gender of nouns/pronouns in New Testament Greek is principally a feature related to the grammatical form of a word and has little to do with the physical gender or sex. Each noun/pronoun has a specific ending according to the gender and case, and this does not necessarily reflect the actual physical gender (sex) of the being or object. Thus, since "Comforter" is masculine in Greek, the masculine pronoun will be used, whereas since "spirit" is neuter, the neuter pronoun will be used. However, this is not the case in the English language, where the pronoun is chosen according to the physical gender of the being referred to. Thus, "He" is used to refer both to "the Comforter" and to the "Holy Spirit" when translating the Greek into English, even though a literal translation would be "it" in the case of pronouns referring to the "Holy

Spirit" or "Spirit of Truth."

Secondly, in most of the instances where "he" occurs in the English version of the verses relating to the Comforter, there is no pronoun in the Greek. That is because the subject of a verb is indicated in Greek by the third person singular form of the verb. It does not distinguish whether the subject is male, female or neuter. However, when translated into English, a pronoun is required and the translators choose the gender of this pronoun according to their understanding of the physical gender of the subject.

Thirdly, the Muslim scholars have failed to acknowledge the fact that, despite the constraints of grammar, when they wanted to add emphasis, the New Testament writers deliberately chose to use the male form of the demonstrative pronoun *ekeinos*, "**He**" /"that one" (male), when referring to the **Holy Spirit.** They did this in order to indicate his distinct personal nature and deity in contrast to an ordinary spirit for which they would have used the pronoun *ekeino*. As we have already explained, the use of "He" here should not be taken as proof that the being referred to is a human being. Let us examine the following verse:

> **John 14:16-17**
> "And I will pray the Father, and He shall give you another Comforter, that He may abide with you for ever even the Spirit of Truth, whom the world cannot receive, because it seeth Him not, neither knoweth Him. But ye know Him, for He dwelleth with you, and shall be in you."

The pronoun "He" which is underlined does not occur in the Greek where it is indicated by the third person singular ending of the verbs, whereas the "whom," and "Him" referring to the "Spirit of Truth" have the neuter endings in Greek to fit with the ending of "Spirit." However, in these verses there is no doubt that the "Comforter" and "Spirit of Truth" are referring to one and the same personal being. By the way, the noun "Truth" has a female ending in Greek. Are the Muslim scholars then going to accept that this passage cannot refer to Muhammad since he was a male?

Let us compare another verse concerning the Spirit:

John 16:13-14
However when He, the Spirit of Truth, is come, He will guide you into all truth; for He shall not speak from Himself, but whatsoever He shall hear, that shall He speak; and He will show you things to come. He shall glorify Me, for He shall receive of Mine, and shall show it unto you.

In this verse, the pronoun "He" that we have underlined twice is the demonstrative pronoun *ekeinos* with the masculine ending. The other occurrences of "He" are required as the subject of the verbs in English but do not occur in the Greek as explained above. The reflexive pronoun translated "Himself" is in the genitive case in Greek in which the masculine and the neuter forms have the same ending.

In any case, whatever our understanding of the grammar, Jesus clearly identifies the Comforter who is coming as the Holy Spirit or the Spirit of Truth. Thus, whoever is the Comforter is also the Spirit. In contrast, nowhere in the Qur'an does Allah address or identify Muhammad as **Spirit** (*Ruh*), nor did Muhammad ever refer to himself as such. According to Qur'an 17:93 Muhammad calls himself "**A man sent as a Messenger**" (*Basharan Rasulan*), not a Spirit.

Qur'an 17:93
Say: "Glory to my Lord! Am I aught but a man, --an
apostle?"

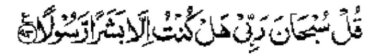

Allah commanded Muhammad to declare his identity
openly and clearly:

Qur'an 18:110
Say: "I am but a man like yourselves,

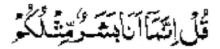

We conclude that Jesus clearly revealed that the
Comforter was the Holy Spirit and not a human being and
therefore he could not be Muhammad.

May God grant us patience and show us the Straight
Way. Amen!

The Divine Teacher

Going back to the Gospel of John, chapter fourteen, let us
see what else Jesus said about the **Comforter**:

John14:26
"But the **Comforter**, who is the Holy Spirit, whom
the Father will send in my name, He shall teach you
all things, and bring all things to your remembrance,
whatsoever I have said to you:"

From this, we can safely say that, the **Comforter** is one who has knowledge of all things. However, in contrast, as we read through the Qur'an, we come across verses that reveal the fact that Muhammad's knowledge was limited.

Qur'an 17:85
They ask thee concerning the Spirit (of inspiration). Say: "The Spirit (cometh) by command of my Lord: Of knowledge it is only a little that is communicated to you, (O men!)"

In the above verse, Muhammad was questioned about the Spirit and clearly, he did not know the answer and therefore had to consult Allah for a reply. However, Allah told him to say that concerning the Spirit only a little knowledge is given to mankind. Muhammad could not answer because like the rest of mankind he had little knowledge on the issue.

On another occasion, it is recorded in the Qur'an that Allah advised Muhammad to consult those "who have been reading the Book." Throughout the Qur'an "the Book" is used to speak of the earlier Scriptures (contained in the Bible) that were revealed to and read by the Jews and Christians

Sura 10:94
If thou wert in doubt as to what We have revealed unto thee, then ask those who have been reading the Book from before thee:

فَإِن كُنتَ فِى شَكٍّ مِّمَّا أَنزَلْنَا إِلَيْكَ فَسْئَلِ الَّذِينَ
يَقْرَءُونَ الْكِتَابَ مِن قَبْلِكَ .....

In effect, Allah is advising Muhammad to ask the Jews and the Christians for anything he has doubts about, because they have read the Book and can teach him. It seems surprising at this point that, if Muhammad is the Comforter, his knowledge is so limited that he has to be taught rather than being the teacher of all things revealed in John's Gospel.

On yet another occasion, some of the Arabs came to Muhammad to inquire from him about their fate in the hereafter. At that time, most of the Arabs believed in the existence of Hell and Heaven and hence the concern of this group. To the utter dismay of his inquirers, Allah commanded Muhammad to say:

Sura 46:9
"I am no new messenger, nor do I know what will be done with me or with you".

قُلْ مَا كُنتُ بِدْعًا مِّنَ الرُّسُلِ وَمَا أَدْرِى مَا يُفْعَلُ بِى

Muhammad had to admit his ignorance on the matter and the fact that he did not even know his own fate in the hereafter. Again, is this not very strange, if Muhammad is the Comforter, when the Comforter is supposed to show us things to come and also to guide us into all truth?

John 16:13
But when He, the Spirit of Truth, comes, He will guide us into all truth…

According to the clear teaching of Jesus, the Comforter is all-knowing and has knowledge of both the present and the future. In stark contrast, Muhammad could not declare the truths about the hereafter. He kept his inquirers in suspense and in doubt as far as their fate in the hereafter was concerned. They wanted words of assurance from Muhammad but he was unable to give them any.

The Glory Of Jesus

Talking about the **Comforter**, who is also described as the "Spirit of Truth," Jesus again said something that is of great interest. Jesus declared:

John 16:14
"**He** shall glorify **Me**."

This reminds us of an occasion when the Apostle Peter declared the glory of Jesus Christ. On that occasion, Peter's declaration came in response to a significant question which Jesus put to his apostles. Let us read:

Matthew 16:13-17 (NIV)
When Jesus came to the region of Caesarea Philippi, he asked his disciples, "Who do people say the Son of Man is?" They replied, "Some say John the Baptist, others say Elijah, and still others, Jeremiah or one of the prophets." "But what about you?" he asked. "Who do you say I am?" Simon Peter answered, "You are the Christ, the Son of the living God." Jesus replied, "Blessed are you, Simon son of Jonah, for this was not revealed to you by man, but by My Father in Heaven…"

For his declaration that Jesus is "the Christ, the Son of the living God," Peter received the blessing of Jesus. Peter's declaration sums up the whole truth concerning the identity of Jesus and it is only **His Father** in heaven who can reveal that truth to whoever wants to know.

In the same manner, John the Apostle also confirmed this truth:

John 20:30-31
"Jesus did many other miraculous signs in the presence of this disciples, which are not recorded in this book. But these are written that you may believe that Jesus is the Christ, the Son of God, and that by believing you may have life in His Name."

When we come to the Qur'an however, Muhammad vehemently objects to Jesus being called the "Son of God." According to the message that he received, a curse will come upon whoever says that Jesus is the Son of God.

Qur'an 9:30
"The Jews call 'Uzair a Son of God, and the Christians call Christ the Son of God. That is a saying from their mouth; (In this) they but imitate what the unbelievers of old used to say: God's curse be on them: how they are deluded away from the truth!"

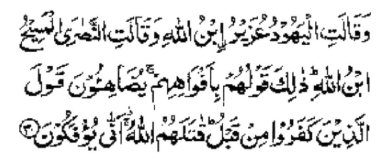

With these words, Muhammad has completely denied the glory of Jesus and the declaration of his Sonship which brings blessing not a curse. Again we must ask, how can the one who is supposed to glorify Jesus, deny his glory as the Son of God?

May God grant us patience and show us the Straight Path. Amen!

The Source Of His Message

John chapter 16 verse 14 further reveals another glaring truth concerning the **Comforter**. Jesus said:

"…**He** shall receive of mine and shall show it unto you".

The Comforter should receive his message from Jesus, and therefore his message should not contradict the message of Jesus Christ in any way.

Did Muhammad receive his message from Jesus? Surely, if it had been from Jesus, Muhammad would not have needed to ask his followers to pray to Allah for them to be shown the straight path that leads to Heaven.

Qur'an 1:6
"Show us the straight way."

For Jesus did not forget to disclose to the whole world that he is the way to the Father in Heaven:

John 14:6 (NIV)
Jesus answered, "I am the way and the truth and the life. No one comes to the Father except through me."

Each of the Gospels gives a detailed account of the crucifixion of Jesus and this was confirmed by Peter, Paul and all the other apostles who preached Jesus crucified.

Acts 2:22-24 (NIV)
"Men of Israel, listen to this: Jesus of Nazareth was a man accredited by God to you by miracles, wonders and signs, which God did among you through Him, as you yourselves know. This man was handed over to you by God's set purpose and foreknowledge; and you, with the help of wicked men, put Him to death by nailing Him to the cross. But God raised Him from the dead, freeing Him from the agony of death, because it was impossible for death to keep its hold on Him..."

From where then did Muhammad receive the following message which completely denies the crucifixion of Jesus?

Qur'an 4:157
That they said (boast) "We killed Christ Jesus the son of Mary, the Apostle of Allah;" –but they killed him not nor crucified him, but so it was made to appear to them, and those who differ therein are full of doubts, with no certain knowledge, but only conjecture to follow, for of a surety they killed him not:--

وَقَوْلِهِمْ إِنَّا قَتَلْنَا الْمَسِيحَ عِيسَى ابْنَ مَرْيَمَ

رَسُولَ اللَّهِ وَمَا قَتَلُوهُ وَمَا صَلَبُوهُ وَلَكِنْ شُبِّهَ

لَهُمْ وَإِنَّ الَّذِينَ اخْتَلَفُوا فِيهِ لَفِي شَكٍّ مِنْهُ مَا

لَهُمْ بِهِ مِنْ عِلْمٍ إِلَّا اتِّبَاعَ الظَّنِّ وَمَا قَتَلُوهُ

يَقِينًا ۞

Let us remember that it was Jesus himself who predicted his own death on the cross and his subsequent resurrection even before the incident happened:

John 3:14 (NIV)
"Just as Moses lifted up the snake in desert, so the Son of Man must be lifted up, that everyone who believes in Him may have eternal life."

John 12:32-33 (NIV)
"But I, when I am lifted up from the earth, will draw all men to myself. He said this to show the kind of death He was going to die."

If Muhammad is the Comforter and the Comforter receives his message from Jesus, why should Jesus turn round nearly 600 years later and tell Muhammad that he was not killed nor crucified. This is unbelievable!

May God grant us patience and show us the Straight Way to heaven. Amen!

Place And Period Of Fulfilment

Dear Reader, let us now look at the command which Jesus gave to his disciples immediately before he departed from them:

Acts 1:4
"Do not leave **Jerusalem**, but wait for the gift my Father promised, which you have heard me speak about…"

The gift they were to receive was the Holy Spirit whom Jesus named the Comforter. In this command, Jesus clearly points out the exact place where the promise of the coming of the Comforter was to be fulfilled. Jesus, without mincing words, pointed to **Jerusalem.** It was **not Mecca,** which was the place where Muhammad was born and where he first proclaimed his prophethood. Can Jerusalem be mistaken for Mecca?

Moreover, on the same occasion Jesus said that the coming of the Comforter would occur in a matter of a few days:

> **Acts 1:5 (NIV)**
> "For John baptised with water but in a few days you will be baptised with the Holy Spirit."

In fact, the coming of the Holy Spirit took place **ten days** later during the Jewish festival that occurred on the Day of Pentecost. It will interest you to know that on that appointed day, even **Arabs** were among the crowd who witnessed and saw the mighty deeds of the Comforter.

> **Acts 2:11**
> "Both Jews and converts to Judaism; Cretans and **Arabs,** we hear them declaring the wonders of God in our own tongue!"

On the other hand, Muhammad was not born until AD 570 and furthermore he did not proclaim his prophethood until AD 610, another 40 years later. That was nearly **600 years** after Jesus made his promise and long after all the disciples that Jesus gave the promise to had died and left this world. The fact is that if Muhammad had met the Arabs who were present on that appointed Day of Pentecost no doubt they would have straightened the records for him.

Power To Believers

A further work of the **Comforter**, whom Jesus called the Holy Spirit, is to give the followers of Jesus power to testify about him.

Acts 1:8
"But you will receive **power** when the Holy Spirit comes on you; and you will be my witnesses in Jerusalem, and in all Judea and Samaria, and to the ends of the earth"

Indeed, the character of the Apostle Peter before the coming of the Comforter was quite different to that after the coming of the Comforter. When a servant girl questioned Peter immediately after the arrest of Jesus, Peter was so fearful that he swore and denied his Lord. On the other hand, when the promise of the Comforter was fulfilled, Peter was not afraid to stand up in the presence of the Jewish rulers and to speak out with boldness:

Acts 4:8-11 (NIV)
"Then Peter, filled with the Holy Spirit, said to them. 'Rulers and elders of the people! If we are being called to account today for an act of kindness shown to a cripple and are asked how he was healed, then know this, you and all the people of Israel: It is by the name of Jesus Christ of Nazareth, whom you crucified but whom God raised from the dead, that this man stands before you healed'"

For Peter had by then received the Spirit of boldness and not a spirit that caused him to fear:

Romans 8:15 (NIV)
For you did not receive a spirit that makes you a slave again to fear, but you received the Spirit of Sonship (adoption). And by him we cry "Abba, Father."

In contrast we read the following concerning Muhammad in the Qur'an:

Sura 33:37
...But thou didst hide in thy heart that which Allah was about to make manifest: Thou didst fear the people...

وَتُخْفِي فِي نَفْسِكَ مَا اللّهُ مُبْدِيهِ وَتَخْشَى النَّاسَ

This verse reveals the condition of Muhammad surrounding the divorce proceedings between Zaid (Muhammad's adopted son) and his wife Zainab. Allah gave a message to Muhammad to disclose, namely that Allah had given Zainab to Muhammad to marry, but because Muhammad **feared** the people, he failed to disclose what Allah wanted him to bring to light. Yet **fear** has no place in the Holy Spirit who is the Comforter.

As we allow the Holy Spirit (the Comforter) to fill us with Power, we shall be seen to be bear the fruit of the Holy Spirit

Galatians 5:22 (NIV)
But the fruit of the Spirit is love, joy, peace, patience, kindness goodness, faithfulness, gentleness and self-control.

This fruit will be seen in our lives towards our fellow human beings.

The promise is exclusive. It is only those who believe in Jesus who can receive **Power** from the Comforter. No wonder the Qur'an declares:

Sura 61:14
...But we gave power to those who believed (in Jesus)...

......فَأَيَّدْنَاالَّذِيْنَ اٰمَنُوْا .....

Every believer and true follower of Christ Jesus is to be identified by this power and the fruits already mentioned. Therefore Allah has no alternative but to raise those who follow Jesus superior to those who disbelieve in him until the Day of Resurrection.

Qur'an 3:55
...I will make those who follow thee superior to those who reject faith, to the Day of Resurrection

..... وَجَاعِلُ الَّذِيْنَ اتَّبَعُوْكَ فَوْقَ الَّذِيْنَ كَفَرُوْٓا
..... إِلٰى يَوْمِ الْقِيٰمَةِ ثُمَّ إِلَيَّ

Christians, who are those who **follow** Christ, are indeed superior for they have power and have also been endowed with mercy and compassion in their hearts.

Qur'an 57:27
We sent after them Jesus the son of Mary, and bestowed on him the Gospel; and We ordained in the hearts of those who followed him Compassion and Mercy.

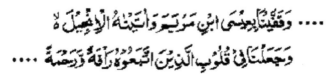

Why do you think Allah has raised those who follow Jesus so high like this as well as giving them **power, mercy** and **compassion?** It is because **Christians** believe and **follow** Jesus, and, above all, have received the **Comforter** into their lives. That is what makes all the difference!

The Bare Truth

We have so far been talking about the **Comforter,** and we thank God, Jesus identifies him as the **Holy Spirit.** Have we any clear grounds for saying that Muhammad is the **Comforter?** A study of the Hadith (The sayings of Muhammad), does not reveal that Muhammad ever claimed to be the Holy Spirit. It is an attempt by modern Muslims to find scriptural support for the prophet-hood of Muhammad.

Furthermore, the Qur'an records that Jesus was strengthened with the Holy Spirit.

Qur'an 2:253
...We gave Jesus the son of Mary Clear (Signs) and strengthened him with the Holy Spirit...

وَءَاتَيْنَا عِيسَى ابْنَ مَرْيَمَ الْبَيِّنَٰتِ وَأَيَّدْنَٰهُ .... بِرُوحِ الْقُدُسِ وَ....

This statement from the Qur'an surely dispels every doubt about the Holy Spirit. He certainly cannot be Muhammad because Muhammad was not born and did not begin his ministry until nearly 600 years after the time when Jesus was being strengthened by the Holy Spirit. The Holy Spirit is none other than the Spirit of God and it is He who Jesus identifies as the Comforter.

From the truths listed above, one can immediately see that the Comforter as promised by Jesus, cannot in any way refer to a human being.

Here are the true facts about the **Holy Spirit**, the **Comforter**. He has been at work since the beginning of creation:

Genesis 1:2
… and the Spirit of God was hovering over the waters

The Holy Spirit came upon people of God in the Old Testament and left them when sin came into their lives. David prayed "Lord do not take your Holy Spirit from me" (Psalm 51:11). Later in the Old Testament, the prophet Joel prophesied that God would pour out His Spirit on all people in the latter days (Joel 2:28). Jesus reinforced this prophecy by saying that, after His resurrection the Holy Spirit would come into the world in a new way and indwell believers until eternity. He would fill men completely with the Power of God. This prophecy was fulfilled on the Day of Pentecost:

Acts 2:1-4
"When the day of Pentecost came, they were all together in one place. Suddenly a sound like the blowing of a violent wind came from heaven and filled the whole house where they were sitting. They saw what seemed to be tongues of fire that separated and came to rest on each of them. All of them were filled with the **Holy Spirit** and began to speak in other tongues as the **Spirit** enabled them."

Explaining the experience on the Day of Pentecost, Peter said that the outpouring of the Spirit in this way was the fulfilment of the prophecy of Joel (Acts 2:14-21).

Dear Reader, the **Comforter** whom Jesus spoke of in the Gospel and who he clearly identified as the **Holy Spirit**, descended on the apostles in the Upper Room in Jerusalem, nearly six hundred years before Muhammad proclaimed his prophet-hood.

Paul upon his conversion into Christianity was also filled with the Holy Spirit, (Acts 9:17). During his missionary journey to Ephesus, he met some disciples and asked them; "Did you receive the Holy Spirit when you believed?" They answered, "No, we have not even heard that there is a Holy Spirit:" Consequently, Paul placed his hands upon them and the Holy Spirit came on them (Acts 19:7).

Dear One, the Holy Spirit can come upon you **today** if only you will believe in Jesus Christ as your Lord and Saviour.

At this time, if you want to give your life to Jesus and then receive the **Comforter**, the Holy Spirit, then join me in this prayer.

My Lord and Saviour Jesus Christ, I thank you for speaking to me through Your Word. I have lived all my past years without you, and have now realised that I am nothing without you. I thank you for your unconditional love for me a sinner, for you shed your blood and died on the Cross on my behalf. Forgive all my sins and cleanse me from all unrighteousness. I sincerely invite you into my life to be my Lord and Master.

I also thank You that You have spoken through Your Word, and have revealed unto me all the truth that I need about the Comforter, whom You sent into the world to abide with us forever.

I now affirm that the **Comforter** whom Jesus spoke about in the Gospels, refers to **none** other but the **Holy Spirit**. I therefore pray and beseech you to fill me with the Holy Spirit in the Name of Jesus, so that I can live for you in Your Power.

Thank you for this wonderful gift in the mighty Name of our Lord and Saviour, Jesus Christ, Amen.